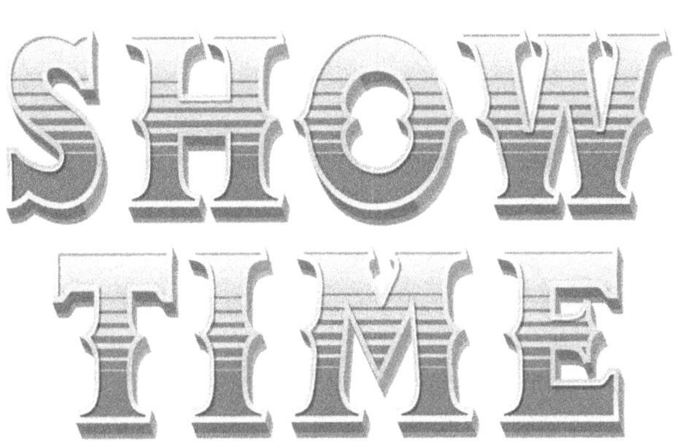

SHOW TIME

A TATTOO ARTIST'S STORY

PYM

This is a story from the sometimes hazy recollections of the author's experiences. The author has made every effort to ensure that the information and timelines are correct and assumes no responsibility for errors, inaccuracies, omissions and inconsistencies. Artistic license has been employed for certain time frames. Real names have been used as a mark of the author's respect for these persons. Other names have been withheld.

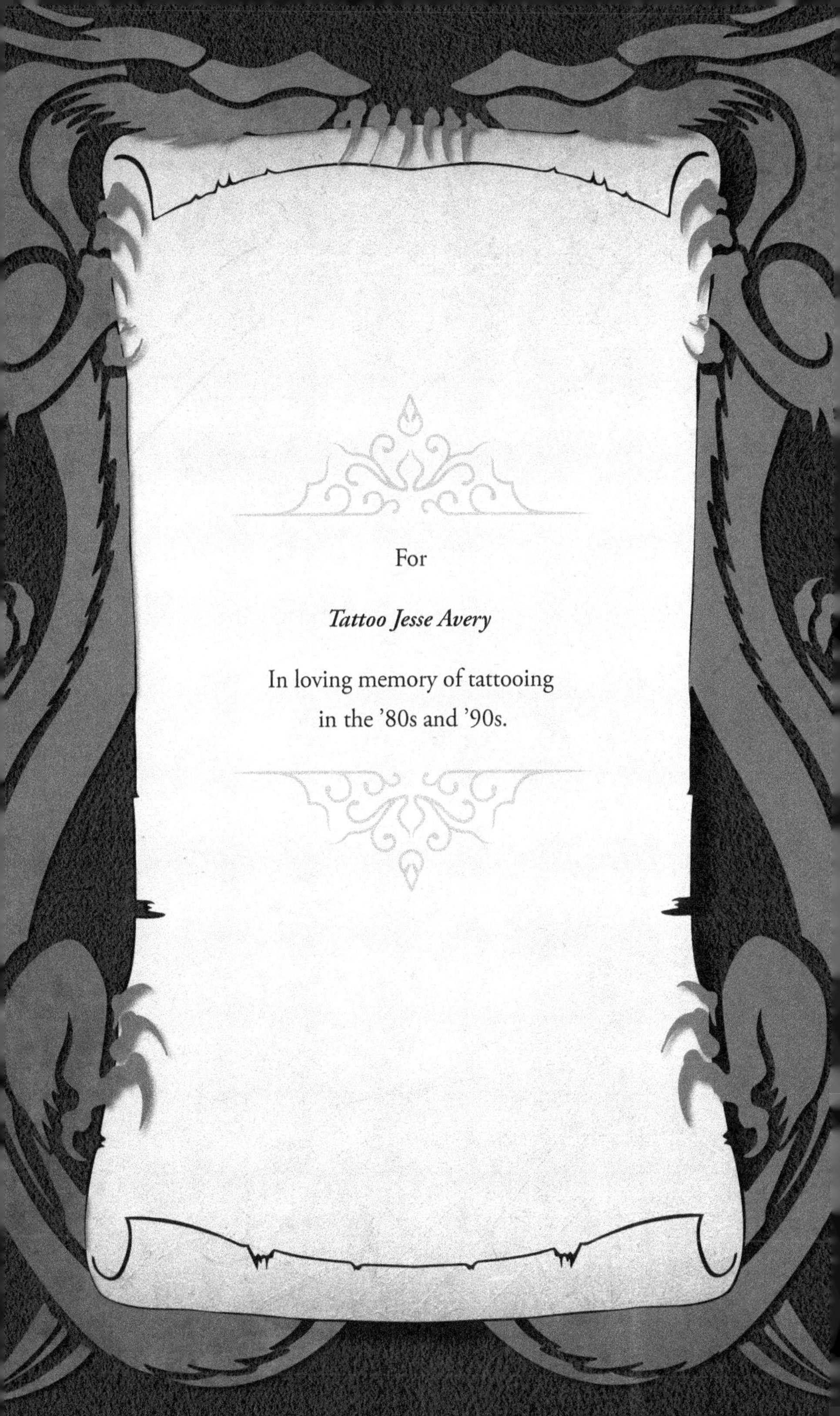

For

Tattoo Jesse Avery

In loving memory of tattooing
in the '80s and '90s.

CONTENTS

INTRODUCTION

People have always asked me how I got into tattooing, and it really is a long story, so I usually fob them off with, 'because the boys all said I couldn't do it', which is the truth in a short sentence. I always wanted to write about it, and it has taken me years to do that.

The long version of the story begins in Finsbury Park, London in 1986, a hotbed of counterculture and activism. Dropping out was in and social unrest fueled the days in the grey weary city. All over England, workers were striking for fair wage, women and gays fought for equal rights and protesters assembled against the unpopular policies of Margaret Thatcher's government. The Queen sat in her Ivory Tower, silent.

I had dropped out of Sussex University in Brighton, where the grand plan had been to study International Law with German and Russian, in spite of my wish to go to art college. In reality, it had been my latest bid to escape my adopted mother. Sussex was the furthest geographical point that I could get to in England, away from her draconian grip. I had just spent ten years in an all girls boarding school after her bid to reform me into a nice young lady failed; she had handed me off to people who had the science down. The years spent in this abusive hell had seemed like a jail sentence. I did my time, internalizing all the anger and hatred because, as I had learnt early on, expressing it just meant some massively demeaning or painful type of punishment. I was on the outside looking in. I belonged nowhere. I had no friends or even allies and a healthy disgust for authority. The cold wet vibe of dissent in London was a perfect fit.

I had met a young gay vegan American woman and was struck by her tales of anarchy and protest and the difference we could make. We joined the women's squatter movement in London and occupied a derelict Victorian house across from Holloway Park Women's Prison. The inmates would reach through the bars and scream obscenities into the night. It was a fitting background for our days supporting the protests against the Public Order Act, marching with activists and students, being pushed into subway tunnels and mercilessly beaten by police armed with truncheons and riot shields. Blood ran in the streets. The IRA planted bombs. Brixton was on fire. War in the street seemed inevitable. It was as depressing as it was exhilarating.

In an alcohol fueled haze, we joined the punks on the Kings Road, making money having our photos taken by American tourists; an extra pound and we would spit for them. Our mohawks melted in the London rain, the bright hair dye dripping down our faces onto our safety-pinned clothes. Women were fiercely resisting the modern popular advertising that girls should look like Kate Moss, thin and pretty and submissive. We were anything but. We learned to fix up the houses we occupied and work on our own vehicles. We wouldn't bow down to orders from men, even Thatcher, whose masculine style of leadership made her even more dislikable. Most of the people I met had a similar mental approach, especially the travelers that came through the squats from time to time.

The English travelers lived in vividly painted old busses and box trucks that had been built out on the inside to live in comfortably. They moved around the country between music festivals and smaller towns. More interestingly, they roamed through France and Spain to escape the cold English winters. I was very intrigued. If I could ever make any money, I would buy one and do the same. The promise of freedom stared me in the face. Eventually, I would travel and tattoo in my own van. I just didn't know that yet.

One day, I found my vegan friend in McDonald's sneakily enjoying a fat juicy beef burger. A big argument about hypocrisy followed and I hopped a train back to Brighton. The squatter scene there was different, the drug abuse was through the roof. There was no excitement, possibility or even chaos, but I had tasted all these things in London. I knew that what I needed was to find the strength and determination to rise above the quicksand of this no hope, no future place.

This is my story of a thousand little things that became one big thing, creating a life of meeting all kinds of people all over the world, taking their dreams and turning them into pictures they can carry with them forever. I always did subscribe to the idea that if you want something badly enough, you will find a way to do it.

This book is intended to inspire and lend strength to the theory that the only limits we have are those that we set for ourselves. It is dedicated to all the people that have been a part of this long incredible journey, good, bad or indifferent. From those I have worked with to those I have worked on, and all the faces in between. I couldn't have done it without you.

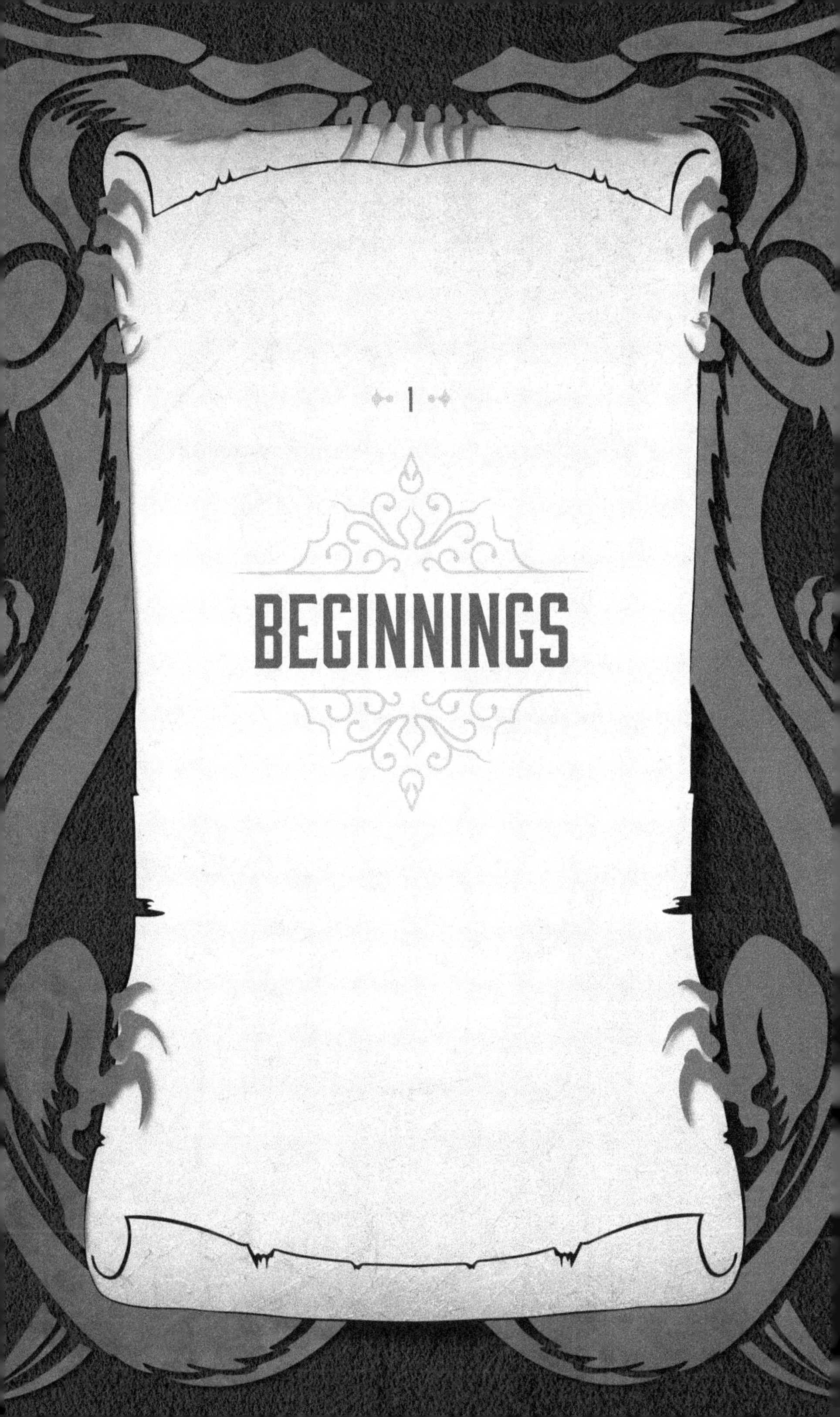
1

BEGINNINGS

The late 1980s is a time that some remember but few can relate to, especially anyone who grew up after the world was forever changed by the iPhone. There were no laptop computers, no cell phones, no social media, none of that. A Polaroid was your instant camera. The phone was attached to the wall and had a cord, so you had to stand right there to use it. It also had a round 0-9 number dial to turn to put in the number, one digit at a time, slowly. A dialing pad was an upgrade. There was no caller ID. There was Directory Enquiries who you would call to get someone's phone number, an operator, and a speaking clock which would indeed, tell you the time. Businesses were listed in the Yellow Pages in alphabetical order so many business names tried to get as close to Aa as possible. Private residences were listed in the White Pages along with address and phone number. Computers still took up whole rooms and were vaguely worried about. Internet for the masses hadn't been invented yet. The Rubik's cube drove us crazy. Music came on a cassette tape or a vinyl record, or the radio. You'd wait for your new favorite song to come on the radio and try to catch it on the first couple of notes by pressing record on the cassette player. Sometimes the DJ would annoyingly talk over the beginning or the end, but you'd make a mixtape of music, like a playlist. Your friends would try to steal it if it was better than theirs. Michael Jackson and Adam and the Ants were cool. Tattoos were for sailors, drunks, ladies of the night and circus attractions. They weren't viewed well.

I was living in a squat in Brighton, England with a bunch of derelict drug addicts who fortunately gave me a lifelong healthy distrust and lack of desire for trying out the finer delights of heroin or methamphetamine; none of the effects looked like fun. I had no desire to sleep on the streets. My parents had given up on me and in those days, moving back home wasn't usually an option. I did too much acid. It was a nasty, messy world. One thing led to another, and soon I found myself at the Social Security Office getting a one-time payout which was just enough to pay for a ticket on the ferry to San Sebastián, Spain. I felt that I'd rather die in a ditch in a foreign country than a drug overdose in a squat in Brighton, England.

Once on the road in Spain, I wandered with my bedroll and starved for a while, sleeping under olive trees and in abandoned buildings, hitchhiking with old men on donkey carts through the countryside. I hadn't thought about it long enough to make a plan or have an itinerary. I didn't know what I was going to do, and I had no money. I discovered Catholic Church missions handing out ham sandwiches and vegetarianism went straight out of the window. I also discovered that being nineteen, slight and blonde was a major attraction for leering truckers and the like, which put a rapid end to my hitchhiking on the main roads.

I needed to figure out what the hell I was going to do, other than just keep myself alive. The answer came by accident one day when I decided to swim across a river to avoid trudging five miles back to the highway bridge to cross it. On the other side there was a small bar where the owner gave my bedraggled cold self a coffee to warm me up and then gave me the bill for it. I told him that I had no money and then looking at a huge bare wall, told him perhaps I could paint a mural on it for payment? I did that then designed him a new menu in trade for food and a place to sleep. Then I painted his cousin's disco walls for money. After that work ran out, I bought chalk and started to do street art on pavement in the local town which paid enough for me to be able to eat.

There are few things more disheartening in this world than having people walk through your art on the street or run strollers through it, so I bought large sheets of paper and used those for my base, anchoring the corners with rocks allowing me to roll them up to take with me ready for the evening's session. Spain had a midday break or siesta due to the daily heat, so everything stopped from noon to 5:00 p.m. and the shops were closed. I chalked religious scenes that I would then sell to the local church for a few pesetas. Through the street art, I met other travelers and street artists and musicians, and we would move in groups between the towns, making a little money for food in the morning and money to travel in the evening. There was more safety in groups. I did that for a while, but all those shenanigans are another story.

There were a lot of English travelers in Spain at the time, and they all had different hustles. They were like a mini, independent sideshow. Some played guitar or drums and sang, others ate fire or did dance and acrobatics. There was always entertainment, no flying begging signs. People gave us money and enjoyed the performances; police moved us on, but there would be a new town and another pocketful of pesetas to be made. It wasn't exactly secure or easy, but nobody cared. I tried to think ahead but there were not many doors open for scruffy traveling types. I learned Spanish drinking coffee and eating tapas in bodegas, talking to the regulars. And then, one day, I heard about the traveling tattoo artist. He was English and traveled and worked in his old Ford van. I was struck by how awesome this sounded. Do art, travel wherever you want in your own vehicle and get paid much more than I could dream of making doing street painting. I needed to find out more and how. I've since read and heard many claims made by people of how they were born to tattoo and all that crap, but I wasn't. I was simply awestruck by the lifestyle and the idea of permanent art; nobody would be able to throw it away or walk across it or paint over it ever again. Of course, he would laugh at me when I asked if he would teach me.

"Girls don't do tattoos," he said. "Don't be stupid!"

There were very few tattoo shops anywhere and it was generally considered that you should take an apprenticeship in order to learn to tattoo properly. To do this, you had to know somebody who maybe knew somebody. If you went into a shop and asked cold, you would be chased out of there with a baseball bat or a machete. This apprenticeship was basically a form of indentured servitude plus constant verbal abuse and, to add incentive, you sometimes had to pay for it. Some apprentices were actually taught a lot of useful things, others just cleaned the toilet, swept the floors and soldered needles for a year. The phrase "you're lucky I don't make you do that with a toothbrush" was commonly applied to the toilet cleaning. Without an apprenticeship, you were a 'scratcher' open to serious harassment by the local tattoo artist who might take your equipment if they found you. Those guys had it just as rough as us women, but a few stuck to their guns and made it to open successful shops. Old school tattooers were a quirky bunch; they held the key to a secret that people wanted, they were a bit scary, and you paid them to hurt you. Most tattooers were bikers, it was just part of the lifestyle. And that's absolutely what it was, a lifestyle. It had nothing to do with being 'cool' and everything to do with tinkering with equipment and building machines and mixing colors and painting flash or design sheets. 'Flash' sheets originated in the carnival days as a way to attract attention, hung up in front of the tattoo artist's booth. Flash cards were used to announce an upcoming act, the 'barker' standing above the crowd and holding up the card with a painting of the entertainer or exhibit.

Oh, and the other thing; no women in tattoo shops!

The only real information about tattooing came from American books like Huck Spaulding's *A-Z Guide to Successful Tattooing* and Spider Webb's *Pushing Ink*, which had only recently been published. Old school American tattooers descended from the carnie or circus days, boardwalks and boweries. In 1891, Samuel O'Reilly had patented the tattoo machine and figured out how to use it most effectively to lay ink in the skin. What line sizes tattooers used, what colors were available to them, and the designs they painted came from their skills as sign-writers and carnie illustrators. It evolved through sailors and wars and the exchange of ideas. The English fine line tattoo style of the 1930s and the American solid thick line style met in the middle and the art refined itself. Many of the designs were specific to the World Wars, for example Death before Dishonor; a woman's tattoo that meant she would be faithful while her man was away and the Hands Across The Water tattoo, symbolizing American and English collaboration in World War II. There were a few female tattoo artists in the American history books, mostly ex-Tattooed Ladies from the circus who had married the tattooer, Mildred Hull, Betty Broadbent, Dainty Dotty, Painless Nell to name a few. In other cultures, women were the tattoo artists; among the Berber in Morocco and in the Philippines, for example, they tattooed by hand. So did Maud Wagner, wife of Gus Wagner and thought to be America's first female tattoo artist. By the 1990s there were quite a few women making a name for themselves as tattooers in North America despite the dominance of men in the trade. They were very serious about their work, the emphasis being on their art, not their appearance. Mostly, the female artists didn't have many tattoos themselves, but a few were heavily covered. There were also tattoo collectors like Elizabeth Weinzirl and Krystyne Kolorful, who were amongst the most heavily tattooed women in the record books.

Madame Vyvyn Lazonga, Judy Parker, Suzanne Fauser, Keely Tackett, Calamity Jane, Kari Barba, Sister Bear, 'Junii' Junko Shimada, Juli Moon, Patty Kelley, Apache Jil, Madame Chinchilla, Winona Martin, Shanghai Kate and Jacci Gresham, America's first African American tattooist, were all names that would become familiar to us in Europe. Many of them owned their own shops. There were also several women who were the wives of bikers and tattooed in their husband's shop. Deana Lippens held the first all-female tattoo convention in Florida in 1998. The women, human beings doing tattoos, were not going to be held back any longer.

England's pioneer Tattoo Lady was Jessie Knight who had grown up as a circus stuntwoman and sharpshooter. She tattooed from the 1940s until the 1980s running her own successful tattoo shops in Southern England and left a massive body of work, which was once displayed in the National Maritime Museum. She would sit on her trunk of designs while tattooing so that no one could steal them. Her tattoos and designs, in the English fine line tradition of the time, were extremely artistic. She was a trailblazer in a world that women couldn't possibly comprehend now; she was slandered and mocked by the men but stood strong and proud despite it all.

The Chinese hadn't begun flooding the world with anything yet let alone cheap tattoo kits. China was just a Communist country tucked in behind Russia on the world map. The Internet as we know it didn't exist. It was as far away as I was in that field in Spain. What did exist were back rooms where tattooists had a needle making station and a place, maybe a shed in the backyard, where they mixed colors; the powder got everywhere; the recipe was top secret. They often built their own tattoo machines and cut their own springs. They ran them hot from car batteries and fiddled with rheostats to convert the AC current to as close to 12 DC volts as possible. The rest of the necessary tattoo supplies, like the actual loose needles which came in wax paper packets of 1000, needle bars, jig blocks and tightening devices, tubes, nozzles and machines were available from suppliers of which there were maybe three or four in the U.S and a couple in England. Everybody knew of everybody else. No way to sneak in unannounced. How could you break into this world of secrets and close-lipped suspicious types, why would you want to? How could you get the equipment? I was completely fascinated with the idea of a trade that you could travel with and make a living and I was going to find a way in.

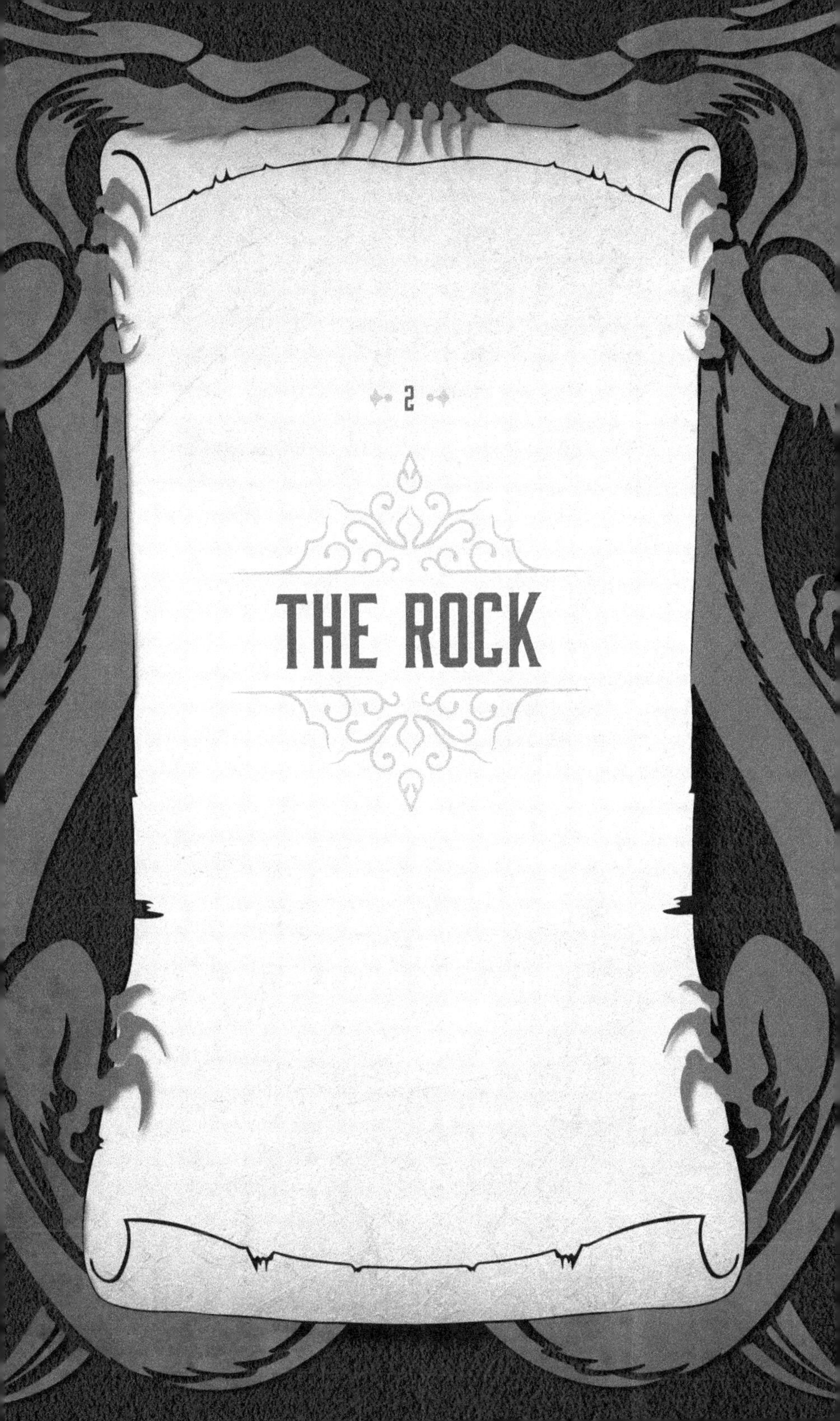

2

THE ROCK

Tacked on the bottom of mainland Spain across from Ceuta, Africa there is a curiously shaped massive chunk of promontory that is visible from miles away. It's an outpost of the British Empire of old and controls the entrance to the Mediterranean from the Atlantic. The Brits have owned it since 1713 and categorically refuse to let it go back to Spain, much to the annoyance of the Spanish. There's a heavily fortified British Navy, Air Force and Army base there and it's commonly known as The Rock. The British military built over 35 miles of tunnels inside the limestone rock during the 1930s, adding up to twice the amount of distance as the roads on the outside. The construction included air raid bunkers and a hospital, food stores, power station and ammunition bunkers. They used the excavated stone to reclaim land, build a submarine base and a nuclear refueling station. NATO aircraft carriers reprovisioned and fueled here after joint training missions. Regularly, there would be thousands of sailors looking for entertainment in the town. The rest of the time, Gibraltar was just one more curious, sleepy town. British businesses had office headquarters to maintain their tax-free identity, tourists visited the Barbary apes (actually macaques) high on the rock and the town was much like any other Empire outpost, shenanigans and all. Legend says that when the apes leave, so will the English.

My trails through Andalucia brought me to the Rock via the Spanish border town of La Línea de la Concepción. The border had been held closed by Spain from the 1960s until 1985, and now a lot of English expats lived on the Spanish side and walked through to work in Gibraltar, or Gib as the locals call it. Thinking that it would be nice to speak English again for a little while and have a decent pub lunch, I walked through the border checkpoint and across the airport runway into the town to investigate. There was a ridiculous number of pubs, and there was also a good wide spot for chalk painting at the top of the main street. I was painting one morning when a man asked me if I could make designs for his stained glass pieces at his studio workshop in town. Different medium, but as long as all the lines joined up to allow for the lead beading, it would be easy enough to figure out. He was making windows for houses and had a big project on deck to make a stained glass atrium piece for a swimming pool in Spain. The money was really good. A month or so later, Her Majesty's Customs turned up, seized my boss, his bank accounts and all of his assets on suspicion of money-laundering and smuggling marijuana from Morocco. They put an enormous padlock on the workshop door and that was the end of that. Another job I had as crew on a treasure-seeking boat headed for Brazil was similarly terminated when the Customs boarded us on a sea trial and discovered a large quantity of Russian arms hidden below decks. Cigar boats full of Gibraltarian duty-free tobacco would regularly run to the Spanish mainland. Smuggling of all sorts of stuff was very popular in this part of the world. Many interesting things could be found whilst beach combing, thrown overboard by boats being chased by the law.

I had got quite used to making a little better money than street painting brought in and got a job in one of the pubs which was how I met the local tattoo artist, Keith Tonna, and his traveling guest artist who was more of a carnie type and spent most of his time on the road tattooing in a mobile studio set up in a large camper van. This was the English tattooer I had heard all about earlier whilst traveling in Spain. His name was Steve Smith. He was here for the arrival of the military's spring training ships and counting on extra tattoo work. Three aircraft carriers docked that weekend. Gibraltar had over 150 pubs and bars in its two-and-a-quarter square mile land area, one tattoo shop and three prostitutes. Odd statistics, you might think, but not when the ships were in, which meant that the U.S. Navy would call in to the port on their way home in huge aircraft carriers packed with thousands of young enthusiastic drunks more than happy to be on shore and spending money after three to six months at sea. Occasionally the English or Australians would join them, once even a Korean ship. Alcohol was very cheap and there was plenty of it. I remember a huge fight between American and Australian sailors in the pub I worked at. The entryway was up a narrow flight of stairs, and the fight created a pile up of unconscious bodies in our only escape route.

At least there was a big solid English oak bar for us barkeeps to hide behind, and heavy glass ashtrays to fend off the drunks that tried to join us until the military police got there.

All the bars were like that when the ships were in, except for one. Charlie's Place on the Castle Steps was a super-seedy, dimly lit joint run by an extremely flamboyant gay man named Charlie who constantly complained about his implanted hair falling out in the shower or chipping his nail polish. He called everybody 'Dahling' and was known for his outrageous drag performances. He was a born Gibraltarian, in his mid-forties, balding and a little paunchy. He had a little fluffy white dog, wore silk suits with brightly colored shirts and gold rimmed sunglasses. He carried an umbrella to protect his skin from the sun. He could have walked right out of a Hemingway novel. He was as bitchy as only a gay man could be, and he lived for the Navy boys coming to town, but he wouldn't put up with any nonsense in his establishment. Charlie's bar was right across the street from the tattoo shop. He would stop by from time to time and tell his outrageous tales. Once there was a sailor just buckling up his belt after a tattoo session when Charlie came in, saying sarcastically that he was pulling his pants on not off. Not skipping a beat, Charlie looked at him, peering down his nose and answered, "Oh that's okay, dear. I like men not boys," and flounced off. Typical drag queen disdain. And the sailors loved him.

Then there were the hookers, or ladies of the night. Two of them came over from Spain to ply their trade and there was one local Gibraltarian girl. One of them was named Maria and the tattoo shop kept several stencils of her name attached to different designs for the poor saps that fell in love with her in their drunken stupor and believed her whispered promises of 'Love you long time.' She would follow them to America when they sent the money, she promised.

I brought the tattooers food after my shift one day during that week and had to squeeze my way through the men sitting and standing on the steps between Charlie's Place and the tattoo shop. I could barely see the artists among all the people crowding the tiny shop. I offered to help next time the ships came in and hold back the drunken hordes while they worked. I thought it might double as a good way into learning something about this elusive trade. Both businesses had a low door with hard stone lintels built to last centuries, so you'd have to stoop to go down the stairs into the basement establishment. Many a drunken sailor would crawl out of Charlie's and stagger across the wide flat step to the tattoo shop, miss the stooping part, smash his face on the lintel and fall in a crumpled heap down the three stairs onto the tile floor bleeding everywhere and demanding a tattoo. If they couldn't stand, they were kicked out, otherwise they would get their tattoo. Everybody was drunk.

The shop was tiny, Keith's workspace was in the back of the room, up a step. It had a small corner set aside for the soldering station and a sink. It was practically dark in there, but he showed me how to wield a piece of cotton thread to tie the bundles of needles, tap the points straight on my fingernail and apply a quick dab of solder, followed by tightening in a jig and attaching to the needle bar. The flux smoke spiraled lazily, making the eyes water and the lungs sting, no ventilation. I will never forget that smell. Occasionally the solder splattered and landed on the skin, making tiny burn holes. Thumbs became calloused from holding the hot needles as the solder melted onto them. Flat needles were the easiest to make. I hadn't encountered magnums yet. Dip in a cup of water to deaden the flux, steam hissing from hot meets cold. I made a lot of needles. The small sink in the corner was for scrubbing all the ink and grease and dried blood off the metal tubes. Toothbrushes and bottle brushes, pipe cleaners and powder detergent, make sure they are clean and then 'cook 'em.' At that time, we were still using dry heat sterilizers and couldn't sterilize the needles which would melt off into a jumbled heap. Needles were twisted off with a pair of pliers after use and the needle bars themselves were sterilized before reloading them with new needles. At a time when tattoo artists were just starting to wear gloves, sterilizing at all was a big advance. Keith was meticulous about cleanliness in his shop and, likewise, Steve, in his traveling van. It was a good thing to learn.

I came to find out more about the basics, the grunt work of the business, the barebones cleaning and preparation that most people learnt through apprenticeships. They categorically refused to apprentice me though, on the grounds that women didn't tattoo; we were destined for life in kitchens. Steve had an apprentice at the time, a British Army soldier named Nick Taylor, who was getting a full back piece tattooed and was relentlessly grilling Steve for information. Nick had a big pool of willing people to practice on and needed pointers. I spent a lot of time being 'busy' in Steve's corner when he came by, trying to understand what things meant and seeing the ink flow from the needles into the skin. Watching a whole tattoo come to life is an impressive thing when it's done well. The outline never looks quite right until it has had it's shading and color applied. The transformation was something special to me. Steve was a very skilled tattoo artist and made the process look effortless. He was also very fast. I watched him lean a young Korean sailor up against a wall once and tattoo an eagle across his entire chest, full color, in two hours whilst standing. Furniture was limited and it was easier for Steve, who was very tall, to work this way rather than have the client lean back in a chair. Tattooing standing up isn't at all easy.

The next spring training port stop came; three American aircraft carriers pulled into the harbor and disgorged thousands of potential customers. Keith and Steve were so busy that they set me up a space in a cramped corner for a couple of tiny tattoos that they couldn't get to and there was no time to mess around or ask questions. Just do it. I suppose that the rationale was that tiny didn't matter if it wasn't tattooed well, and they were drunk anyway. I was nervous and sweating and shaking throughout the entire process, but I had done tattoos. In a shop.

The guys had forgotten that by the next day though and we went back to status quo. I was the scrub, I cleaned floors and fetched lunch. I think that they hadn't actually believed that I could or would rise to the challenge of tattooing the sailors with absolutely no clue of how to do it. Hopefully someone fixed those tattoos later.

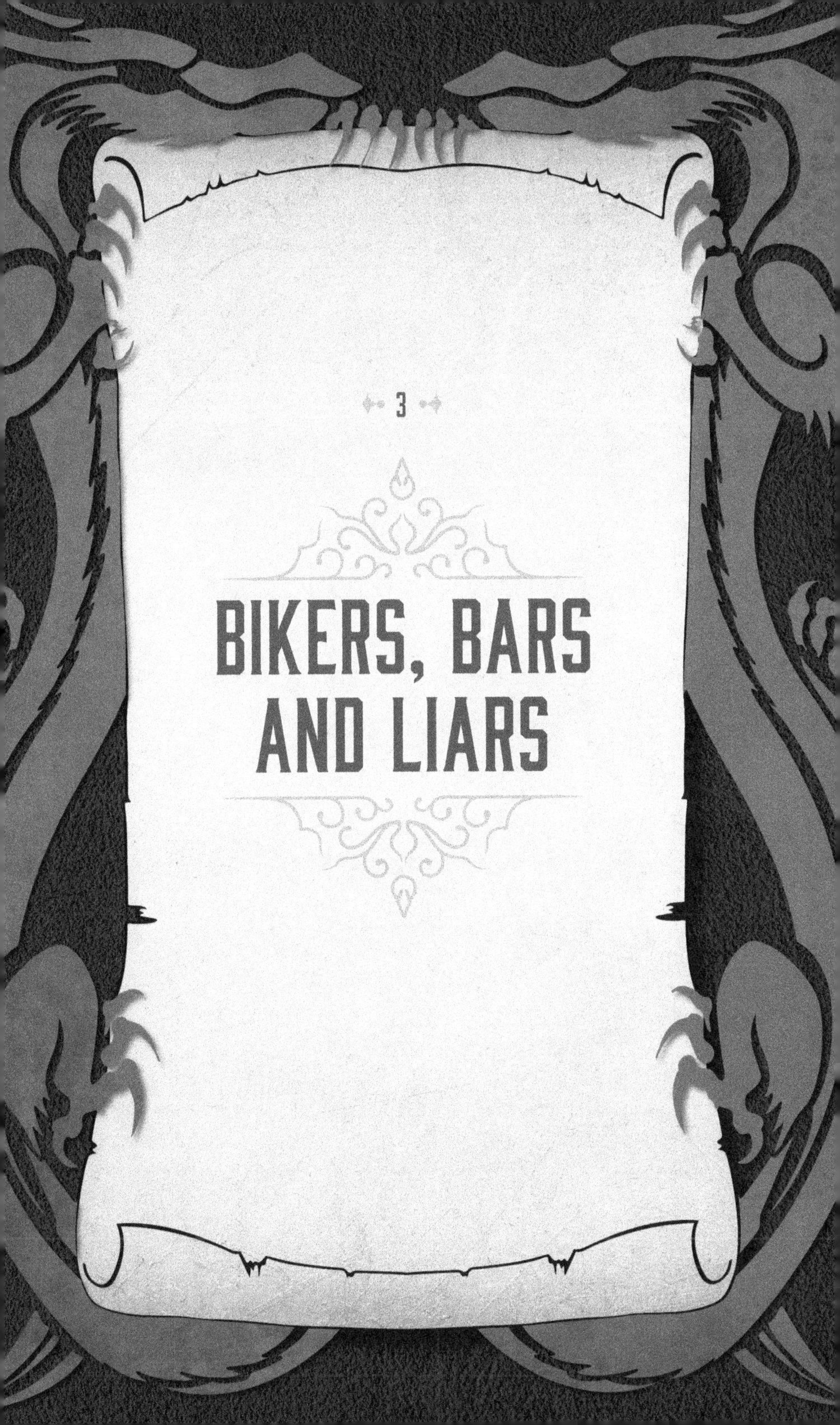

BIKERS, BARS AND LIARS

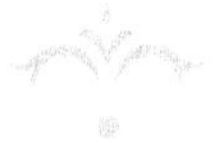

ow I was on a mission.

Becoming a tattoo artist was going to require equipment and that meant real money. Gibraltar was on a lull until next year's spring training fleet, so I went back to England. First, I bought a motorcycle. This seemed to be a pre-requisite for being a proper tattooer, plus it doubled as transportation. I had ridden scooters and minibikes before so I thought it would be easy enough to ride this bigger machine. I found a BSA Bantam 175, paid for it and got the paper and keys. Then I asked the seller to show me how it worked, at which point he insisted he couldn't sell me the bike if I didn't know how to ride it.

"Too late, mate! Now if you could just kindly show me how it works…"

I wobbled home mostly in the gutter and a few days later was happily racing around all over town.

I found several jobs, one at a local pub behind the bar, and two others delivering sandwiches and working in a café. The pub brought insights into the local tattoo shop, Skin Deep, which was just down the street and I pretended to know nothing, just asking dumb questions. Besides, the owner was an intimidating skinhead who went by the name Nutty Dave and had a reputation for fighting as well as incredibly clean tattoos. The punters, or customers, proudly showed off their new work and talked about how great Dave was and the work really was good. Bright, bold and solid. Dave Ayres didn't draw, wasn't an artist in the true sense of the word, but he could tattoo the hell out of any design and add his own flair. I have met a few tattoo-ers like that over the years and I know what they meant, back in the day, that often being too artistic just gets in the way. It means that you get caught up in trying to make a design more frilly when all it requires is solid basic bones. It's a fine line to distinguish and depends a lot on the design in question, but some aren't meant to have frills. The other jobs were really just to pad my pockets because £2 an hour cash wasn't much and at 60 hours a week, I was dog-tired most of the time. But the money I had saved was finally enough to get the tattoo supplies I needed and now it was time to pull off the hardest part.

There were two main supply companies in England at that time and I had ordered enough things during busy times at the Gibraltar shop to be a bit familiar with the owner of one of them so it was time to attempt to place an order of my own, having snuck the phone number and maybe an old catalog out of the shop in Gib. Nothing too suspect about ordering what basically amounted to a starter kit then, eh? I fumbled a bunch of coins into the slot in the telephone box and crossed everything I had.

"Umm, yeah, so I would like to order a shader and a liner machine, needles, bars, tubes, ink and a power pack and clip-cord …please."

Eric Davis had a lot of questions, most of which were easy enough to field like needle grade, spring cut, tip size and then came the final wrap up.

"Just send it to the usual address then, mate?" He asked.

"Ummmm no. I was going to just get it sent here to me and then take it with me seeing as I'm going south soon anyway, and I can deliver it to them for less…" I was shaking.

"You sure you're not pulling one on the sly then, mate?" Eric chuckled.

"Me, no, never!" Sweating in the cold, damp phone box.

"So, if I called down there, they'd okay it?"

"Well, yeah, of course, it's their order…"

It was so hard to keep it together, it was like being interrogated by the border police; hardest lie I have ever told, mostly because everything depended on it. Please just say yes. A long silence followed.

"Alright then, what's the address? Cash on delivery." I almost yelled aloud with relief.

He took the details.

"Good luck, mate, make sure you keep ordering from me, mind. I put you on the List."

I hung up and slumped back against the side of the phone-box.

I had made the almighty List; I could buy supplies. I was IN… and he had known. To this day, I really don't know how I got through that phone-call. Maybe because I knew what I needed which was actually half the battle. Who knows. I did seem to run on more luck than judgement in the early days. I ordered from Davis Tattoo Supply until I left Europe thirteen years later.

I quit all of my current jobs and started hanging out at a biker pub on the other side of town in case Dave found out. He wasn't a biker then. I made friends with lots of people who liked tattoos and started painting signs and murals to make money. Once the tattoo kit came, it would be time to move on to the next part of the puzzle, so I gathered information and had some fun on my bike at the expense of the nerves of car drivers. I hoped to put England in the rear-view mirror once and for all. I've never enjoyed being cold and wet and miserable.

It took almost a month for the supplies to arrive and I had almost given up on them. As soon as they were delivered, I worked on getting everything ready to use. I sat in the freezing cold house. I was renting a room from a friend who didn't believe in heat. I made batches of needles until my fingers couldn't move anymore. I mixed colors in the kitchen and made a ridiculous mess. I played with the tattoo machines, tuning them up and tattooing my own leg until the roommate complained about the buzzing noise in his head. And then, I went to the pub. I had to park my bike halfway up a hill for starting purposes; the battery was almost dead, I couldn't afford a new one, and the bloody cold wasn't helping it hold charge. Alternator or starter out, wasn't sure. I planned to rebuild it when it warmed up a bit. The weather was enough to freeze the balls off a brass monkey, or just brass-monkey weather, in the colloquial. I went to the pub with the closest convenient slope for second gear start de-clutching by myself. Not many hills in this town. I walked down to the pub and was happy to see that my usual stool at the bar closest to the fireplace wasn't taken. A good opportunity to thaw out my fingers.

I don't remember the pub's name anymore: King's Head, Queen's Head, Nag's Head, Chelsea Inn? All English pubs were pretty much the same. It was like walking into a cave, just the dimmed lights on the wall like old torch-bearing holders and the bar, sparkling against one wall, softly calling 'come hither; I hold the delights you seek.' Of course, it was a bit more colorful than usual because it was almost Christmas and the tinsel and Yuletide cards cascaded down from the overhead mantel, twinkling green, yellow, red and blue. Good old Christmas, nothing like that time of year to drive a person to drink. The overall room décor was dark, usually wood paneling at least halfway, sometimes all the way up the walls and the bar was solid wood with a mirror across the back to magnify the bottles of liquor stacked there next to the upside-down, shot-measuring mainstay bottles of the most popular cheap crap. Pictures on the wall of really old painted landscapes, fox hunts and the like in big elaborate frames. There's always a fireplace, because most of England gets cold and dank most of the year and the tables and chairs are the solid kind, victims of many fights and falling down drunks, the good old 'local.'

I asked the barmaid for a pint of lager. The usual chit chat, how's yer life, how's the job going, all that. Conversation with barmaids was pretty much obligatory. I knew this from previous years working the pubs myself. Tending bar was like being a free psychologist for the lonely old or the depressed young men that would post up from opening and whine about their miserable lives or their bitch of an ex-wife or whatever malady, or even just the bloody weather. The occasional woman. You would try to find any excuse to walk away: polishing glasses for the millionth time, imaginary specks of dust, inventory for the boss. Problem was, there was always more than one, drowning their sorrows at different corners of the bar. Looking for excuses to get your time.

"What kind of crisps you got then?" (Well, they're all hanging on the bloody wall right there, as you well know and can see, and you always get cheese and onion so….).

"Same as yesterday, John."

"Oh, cheese and onion then."

About enough to drive a person crazy, but they filled the gaps between lunch crowd, off work lads and evening punters. They all needed attention, and you knew way more about them than you ever wanted or needed to. Good training for handling the general public, as it would turn out. But it took some control not to get aggravated with them. I passed the time of day with the barmaid briefly, sitting at the old bar, ripples of light spinning off the bottles stacked behind the till and the stemmed glasses swaying gently up above in their spots as the bartender washed and dried and hung them up. Pint glasses in the wire baskets by the sink, then onto the mats under the bottles, ready to sling under a beer pull when the punter ordered. My fingers traced the dents and divots and carvings in the varnished surface behind the bar mat, actual cloth mats from the brewery to soak up the beer spills. The sour smell of old yeast was vaguely familiar, the woodsmoke from the fire and lemon wood oil. My finger hit a patch of sticky dried up soda…well, hopefully. The stories a place like this could tell would probably boggle your mind. I'd been privy to too many myself.

It was end of the day shift, 8- 4 or 9- 5 depending on what you did for a living, and people began to meander in, filling up the empty chairs and tables and barstools. Regulars in their usual spots, kicking out anyone who didn't know better, sometimes standing and mean-mugging, sometimes just stating, "you're in my seat, mate."

The bartender got busy. I started to go through my pockets to find pencil and paper to make notes for the next day's mural job and stacked some of the contents on the bar mat next to me as I dug deeper. Rotten pencils, always disappearing. A man I didn't know sat down on the stool next to me and was observing the whole thing.

"What's that then?" he asked as I laid down the measuring tape.

"It's a measuring tape", I replied evenly. "I've been told all my life that this is nine inches (gesturing a three inch-ish gap between finger and thumb), so I thought it was time to find out. Seems a bit off to me."

Somebody standing behind us laughed. The man gave me a 'fucking arsehole' look and went back to his beer. The person laughing said "she got you, mate!" and I turned to see one of my biker friends. His name was Frog, a tall, tubby around the middle, young chap who I rode with often when we had nothing better to do than race around town, cutting off cars and kicking the mirrors off the cars that tried to cut us off. He had long greasy black hair and a sparse goatee but was mostly friendly and most definitely had my back. He would get the odd girlfriend who didn't believe that we weren't shagging on the sly and have to not talk to me for however long that lasted. Frog said that he had just stopped by my house to see if I was there and that my roommate, Dave, had told him I had been busy all week making a mess and stinking up his house, something about buzzing noises and then he had wobbled off in his methadone cloud, mumbling all the while. Dave was cool, he just could never outrun the drug habit that the doctors had given him, despite the fact that the motorcycle wreck which had almost killed him had paid off the house.

"Sumfink good then?" he asked.

"Tattoo set up came."

Suddenly I had a lot of interest from the regulars and a seemingly endless row of beers started to flow towards me.

"I want to be first."

"When are you starting then?"

"How much, mate?" And on with the questions. Perfect. Nothing like the good old local for some free advertising. It looked like it would be a busy weekend.

⊷ 4 ⊷

KITCHEN MAGIC

ow that I had people to actually practice on, the next part of the puzzle was to figure out where I was going to do the tattooing. I couldn't tattoo at the house I lived in because my roommate wasn't a 'people' kind of person. I didn't have any apparent alternative than to go to my customers' houses and work on them there. The price was right. This first wave of practicing would be free. Everyone who had asked for tattoo work knew in no uncertain terms what they were getting themselves into but, somehow, their trust went beyond the realm of reason at points. A few of the designs were definitely way above my pay grade at that time, but they insisted to the point that I would have lost the opportunity if I kept saying it was too complex. They gave me their addresses and I turned up at the set time to do their tattoos. The layout of every place was different, the first half hour spent assessing where in the house and how best to set up to work. Bigger kitchens were preferable, the surfaces being cleanable with a large table away from the food preparation area. I would later hear of home tattooers 'sterilizing' their tattoo equipment in dishwashers, but that seemed incredibly suspect to me. If the living room had a table or space for two chairs, that worked too. Most of the people I knew lived in bedsits (studios) or rented a room. We would always find the best way to make it work, although it wasn't always easy. I rapidly gained an appreciation for proper furniture and an ability to make the best of a small space.

There has always been a certain routine and basic set up for the actual process of doing a tattoo. There needs to be a barrier of some sort between the clean materials and the workspace. Usually this is some type of plastic wrap because the surface will quickly become contaminated with biohazard. Biohazard is created by contact with human blood or bodily fluids. Spray bottles of soapy water for cleaning the skin as you work require a disposable bag over them and clip cords should be wrapped too, as you'll be touching them with gloves when changing machines. Anything that is constantly touched throughout the process and is not single use should have a disposable cover. Single use items are laid out and then assembled on the barrier surface. A disposable cup of rinse water is poured and set ready to use. Colors poured into their little upended cups. Vaseline to smear on the skin. Razor to shave the area to be tattooed. All of this will be wrapped up and disposed of after the tattoo is finished.

Maybe you can't envision the numerous disasters waiting to happen just with the basic layout. As the years and disasters tick by, everyone develops a method which works best for them. I use a smoothly finished A4 sized piece of stainless steel as my work tray, wrapping it with cling wrap. This prevents the wrap from migrating off to wherever it feels like with the slightest pressure or tug, taking everything piled on top of it along for the ride. Some artists use plastic trays or dental bibs, it's all personal preference. I use a coffee mug to set my rinse cup in because the slightest tap on the rim of a plastic rinse cup will spill its contents everywhere. This water becomes biohazard as soon as it has been used to dip, even once, any needle that has had contact with the body fluid of a client so when it is spilled the clean up is significant. I tap the little color cups in vaseline so that they stick to the surface of the work tray and don't wander off when the color is poured into them. A bunch of little things that make life easier.

That's just a small part of the set-up process. Needles now go into tubes and the tubes are fed into the machines. Don't snag or bur the needle in the tube, make sure it's angled right, turned the right way on the bar. Attach the needle bar to the armature bar, not too snug, not too loose. Tear the glove finger that got snagged in the process. Replace the glove. Hopefully your hands aren't sweaty.

Now seat the needle for the right depth into the skin, clamp the tube in place. Don't crush the tube, but don't leave it loose enough to slide with the vibration of the machine. Maybe it won't tighten enough. Problem solving is a constant. Nothing ever goes 100% problem free. Ever.

Now try all that with an audience. Or better yet, as a total rookie in someone's bedsit (English for bedroom, seating area and kitchen all in one) with horrible lighting and a tan carpet. Awful lighting has always been a huge challenge for tattooing. From shops in basements to convention floors the lights are often fluorescent yellow and far away from the work surface. In short, if you don't have a portable, bright light source, it's very hard to see what you are doing. You will often be working half upside down in your own shadow in a dimly illuminated corner if you don't plan in advance. In the '80s portable lamps with daylight bulb lights were not yet invented, a desk lamp was about as good as it got. So now you are trying to maintain some semblance of cool in a dimly lit bedsit with a crumpled heap of badly smoothed out cling wrap sort of taped to a greasy vinyl kitchen tablecloth with your tattoo equipment laid out and all this seems so far from that shop environment with the shiny surfaces and the tiled floor.

It's time to shave and clean the skin and apply the transfer.

For the uninitiated, the transfer is the traced basic lines of the tattoo design which have been either run through a transfer machine or thermal copier or in my case, hand traced on stencil paper, to transfer carbon color to the skin so that you can trace the line work with the tattoo needle. The color of the applied stencil is usually purple. There are only a few liquids in this world which will allow for the proper application of the stencil, but they must be neither too wet nor too dry at the exact moment of contact with the skin or the transfer will not happen correctly. You might get two, possibly three, attempts out of one stencil unless the paper becomes too wet and disintegrates in your hand, leaving a mushy purple smear all over the customer's body part. If the skin surface is too dry, only half the stencil transfers. Now all the purple must come off the skin in order to reapply the stencil because otherwise all the lines and smudges meld into an illegible mess. A very purple mess. Rubbing alcohol is the only thing that will remove the stencil attempt. Did I bring rubbing alcohol? Pretty soon everything is purple. Transfers, while very useful, can also be a complete nightmare and very difficult to deal with. In the case of intricate four-inch-wide Celtic knot work bands, they are completely necessary, but trying to match up the lines of a design formulated on a flat surface and then applied to what amounts to a tubular or uneven body part is an almost impossible feat requiring immense patience, multiple stencils and a lot of rubbing alcohol.

And then, there is always the fact that the client may not like the placement or may want to see what it looks like somewhere else. I always maintain that I can tell if the client is happy just by the look on their face when they first see the image in the mirror. If they look for too long, it isn't right. Do it again. (For the record, the customer is always wrong).

What about size? The design always looks much bigger on a flat, white piece of paper than it will on the skin. To resize designs in the '80s meant redrawing the whole thing as home copiers cost roughly the same amount as rent. For this reason, many tattoo shops had cabinets full of the same design in multiple sizes. The scratcher was not so lucky. Once the transfer has finally been successfully applied and everyone is in agreement (including the client's accompanying artistic director and other support entities), then the business of actually applying the tattoo may begin.

And now to the use of furniture. The tattoo artist and client both require a chair for most tattoos, except when the tattoo is on the leg or foot or pretty much anywhere south of the Tramp Stamp (lower back) area. A flat surface is required for this so that the client can lie down and ideally it should be at the right height for the tattooer to be able to reach the design without bending over too far, the equipment and ink being at table height. This can be problematic and especially in circumstances where a massage table is not readily available. If possible, joining three armless chairs together in a row would work, a tattoo convention trick. Or laying them on the picnic table provided at a motorcycle rally. A kitchen table might not take the weight of the client and it is already in use as a work surface. Dilemma. Likewise, tattooing an arm would require resting it on the tattooer's lap at the time. Improvised. Not ideal. Some clients would get the wrong idea. Manhandling of body parts and the furniture in play was and still often is, absolutely not good for the tattooer's posture. Even in the best scenario, it is still the tattooer who has to wind around in awkward positions to best reach the body part. Necks, chests and stomachs are some of the most difficult areas to reach. I remember wondering why all the old-timers walked with canes and wore ridiculously thick glasses. Now I know.

We are ready. The kitchen table is laid out with all the necessary equipment. The lighting is abysmal. There are two same-height chairs. The stencil has finally been applied on the outer forearm. The tattooer must cross her legs to get the forearm even close to high enough for her to properly be able to reach the tattoo, a towel over her knee. Pick up the loaded machine, insert the clip cord and press the foot switch. Nothing happens.

Press again. Still nothing. For the experienced professional, here begins a process of calmly tracking down the problem. Check the connections. Make sure that the power pack is actually switched on or properly plugged in. Try a different machine. OK, it's the machine. Check for shorts. Check for broken wires or springs. Check to make sure the needle bar isn't too tight or that the spring hasn't moved away from the contact screw. And the number one thing that newbies never ever find, a tiny piece of hair between the spring and the contact screw. Stressed, frustrated and sweating profusely, the inexperienced tattooer unloads the other machine (because we tested it and it worked) and loads the liner tube. The machine now works, but differently because it is set up as a shader. No time for all that right now, let's get this show on the road. Grab the customer's arm, stretch the skin tightly by holding the back. Dip the needle in the black ink. Apply the needle to the skin to trace the purple line. A huge black blob of ink wells up at the bottom of the needle and you can't see the needle or the line you're supposed to be following. Wipe with a piece of paper towel (I once heard of a person using socks to wipe his tattoos.) But you forgot to smear the skin with vaseline before you started so the black smudge isn't going anywhere, in fact it's halfway across your stencil now. Spray soap and water. Wipe. There went half the transfer. And the customer hasn't stopped talking and moving all this time.

Still want to be a tattoo artist?

For some of us, being a kitchen magician or scratcher or any other number of insulting names was a rite of passage. We wanted to learn and there was no other way to do it than tattooing your friends in your house or theirs. If you got really lucky there would be three dogs playing, a screaming baby and some drunk regaling everybody with tales of his prison stint and telling you how to do the tattoo all in the same space where you were trying so hard to concentrate. The goal was to find a way from here to a shop, having just enough of a clue to be useful to the shop owner, and then you could actually learn in a professional environment and get a whole lot better at tattooing quickly. Some people never follow that path, and they are the true scratchers.

As an example, Fat Cat Tattoo in California with its multiple locations worldwide was started by Christopher Aguilar in the '90s, a tattooer with the same start described here. It requires a strong will to do better, without help from the professionals and their apprenticeships. People who claw their way up from this place never forget where they came from.

I didn't cover the stress of the responsibility of permanent marks and the amount of sleep you can lose when you aren't happy with the results. It's always been easy to talk a good tattoo, evidenced by the scratchers parading their customers around bars to show off some ghastly work, talking all the while about how amazing it was. Were we looking at the same thing?

But you have to persevere and above all, maintain the bluster and the showmanship…right up until the ship has sailed far from port.

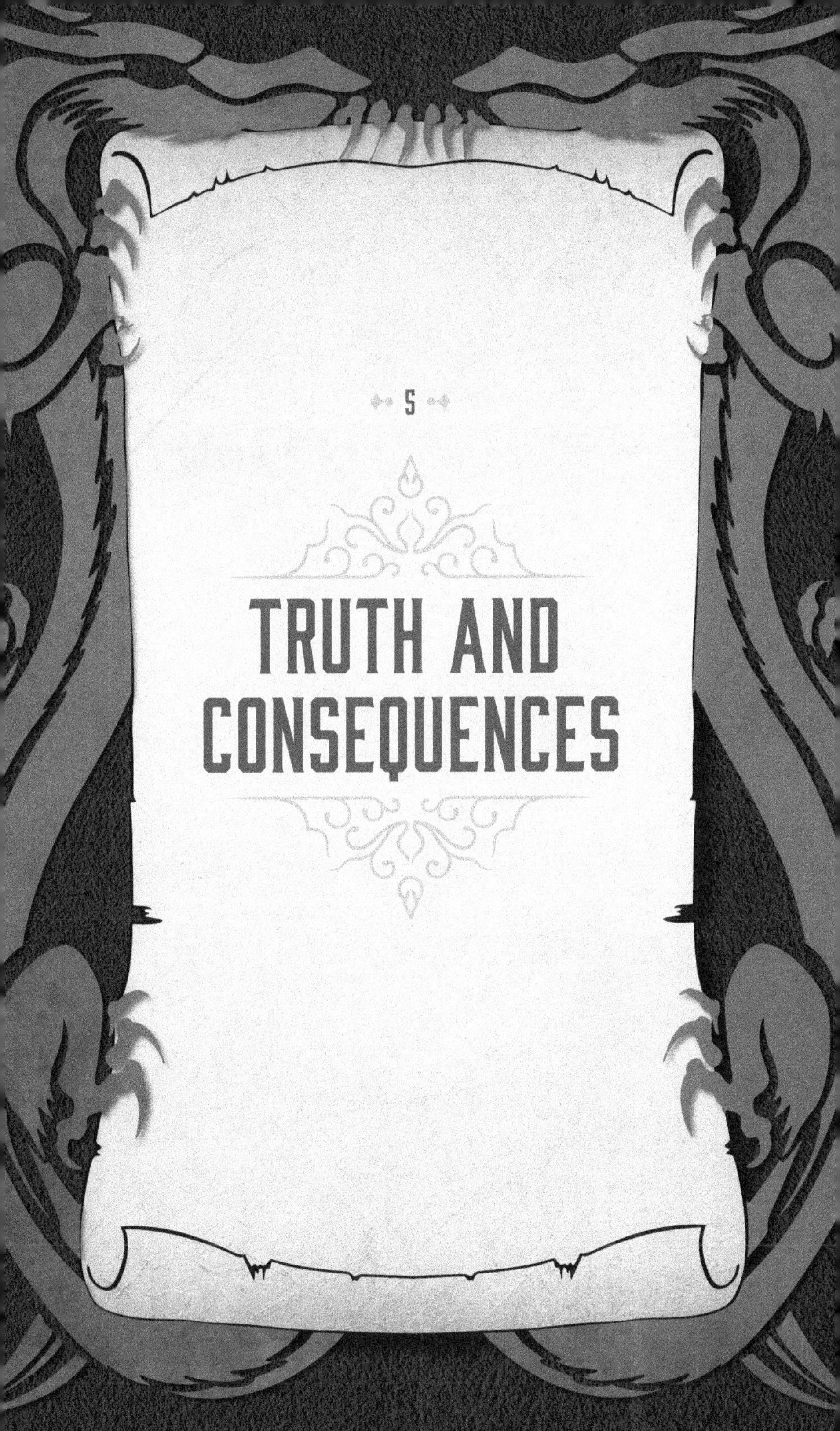

TRUTH AND CONSEQUENCES

 spent a few months tattooing and gathering a little experience, mostly of how not to do things. It felt like I was beating my head against a brick wall. I was fortunate to have enough artistic ability to carry me through the technical difficulties, at least until the tattoo healed and was a little weathered. Normally, it will take at least six months to settle into its permanent version. Almost every tattoo can look just fine when it is freshly done, but as it heals and lines or color fall out or the black spreads under the skin, it can become something vastly different from the original. I have seen tattoos that caused massive scarring on people, others that literally fell out most of the way and yet more where the color or black migrated under the skin almost irreparably. Over the years, I would become skilled at covering or fixing up old and unrequited tattoos and see many and terrible things done to skin. Sometimes, awful tattoos would come from other shops. The most scandalous one that comes to mind was down the street from where I worked in Montreal. The owner would hire scantily dressed women with zero experience in tattooing, the only job requirement was to

be provocative and sexy. The girls tattooed men who were look-ing at everything on display except for artwork and didn't real-ize how bad their tattoo was until they had paid and left the shop and taken off the bandage. We fixed a lot of those, some-times the same day.

Of course, at the time that I was learning, I was just contrib-uting to the problem because I had no technical input. I knew the signs of lines that would not last, as the red welt with no ink in it was pretty easy to spot. Trying to re-apply the line meant good lighting and a steady hand, sometimes more of a disas-ter than just leaving it to be touched up after it healed. Other lines would blur, showing instantly that they were too deep; no fixing that, maybe shade up to the edges and try to conceal them within the tattoo. The crispy, clean black line was elusive. The recipe for success was hidden in the secret world of tattoo shops and forbidden apprenticeships. Snippets of information came through here and there, but mostly the learning was done the hard way. It all had to do with the tuning of the machines, the types of needle groups and how they were soldered, depth of the needle and throw of the machine as well as the compo-sition of the ink and the type of skin you were working on. A lot to learn. And that was just for the lines. The only thing that wasn't secret was the fact that clean solid lines were the mark of a good tattoo and were the most important part to get right.

The beginning was very heavy going and even with the input I had had at the Gibraltar shop there were still so many unan-swered questions. It was common practice for professional tat-tooers and those with the coveted apprenticeship to mock those of us who had chosen to teach ourselves. But I can tell you, that at least for me, the biggest difficulties of all were reliving the tattoo experience after the client was gone, the frustration of not being able to get things right and the vision of a terrible tattoo on the person's skin. Often, as it turned out, the result really wasn't that bad, but the search for perfection is a long and rocky road and not for the faint of heart. I tore myself apart constantly, but still could not stop trying.

Tattooing is a strange mistress. Despite all the pitfalls and hurdles, we strive to figure it all out and finally be happy with the outcome of the work, a rare achievement for most artists, even years into their craft.

I had very few designs available for people to look at but mostly, customers gave me a picture of what they wanted on a crumpled piece of paper. I also had sketchbooks full of my own drawings. Eventually I would become a custom design artist, which means that whatever I draw for my client does not come copied from mass design sources. I also learned to draw freehand. Freehand designing on the skin allows for the use of the whole body as a canvas, even if you are only working on a really small part of it. You can bend and wind the lines around the body's natural curves and make the tattoo move with its wearer, popularly for example, the wings of creatures tattooed on the shoulders. Front or back. Put the client in front of the mirror and tell them to move their arms up and down. Flight! Freehand is very useful for tribal designs and cover ups and large Japanese designs, anything that involves filling in an empty background area on the body. It's important to master the technical aspect of tattooing before you can be a competent freehand artist though, concentrating on art as well as technique can be a giant rabbit hole.

I finally started to make a little headway, if it's not difficult you aren't learning. Spring was coming. My plan was to go back to Spain and begin my career as a traveling tattoo artist. I knew that I was far from a professional but hopefully I could learn more by simply working and meet new tattoo artists who might give me a bigger welcome than the one I was currently enduring. The more tattoos I did, the more messages came down the line from the local tattoo shop owners that I had better knock it off, or else. They would see fresh tattoos on people and ask where they had got them done, not recognizing the style as being from one of the local shops. It was time to move on before I had my equipment removed from my possession.

I sold my motorcycle to raise the money to buy a van. Or more accurately, a Commer van, the kind the English used for weekends in the country, similar to a Volkswagen bus. It was green with a snub nose and double back doors that opened outwards, a roof that lifted up so that one could stand up in it and all the camper van trappings which made it very high end compared to my last mobile dwelling. It had a working sink and water tank, a gas stove that was less likely to explode in my face than my last one, inbuilt storage cupboards, a seating area that became a bed when the table was disassembled and another sleeping area across the front bench seat. Even little curtains that wrapped all the windows. It had easily cleanable melamine work surfaces within close reach of the seating, and little electric 12-volt lights above them. It was perfect.

I got to work immediately fitting out the van, adding a battery for in-line charge so that I would have a constant 12-volt DC power source at my workstation for running my tattoo machines. Direct DC battery power is the smoothest for running machines and eliminates the need for an AC transformer. The biggest difference in operations would mean tuning all the tattoo machines to function for their specific jobs on 12 volts. This actually made life a lot easier for me, removing a lot of variables from the scenario. Until that point, the goal had been to tune them to a rheostat, the power variable had been 0-20 volts. Removing options meant a more delineated target for me. The batteries would recharge when the engine was running. I would have to swap the clip cord connector cables out when my work battery became low. Electricity has always been a mystery to me, and I wasn't smart enough to put in a switch system, but it was easy access to the battery box under the work area. The only drawback was that the battery box was metal, and I once got shocked badly enough to throw myself out of the back of the van when I accidentally clipped it with the positive terminal. I only did that once. I bought a small field autoclave that would sit on the gas stove for sterilizing. The little Commer was loaded with my tattoo equipment, and I was more than ready to leave England.

Heading to the ferry terminals in Dover was always exciting to me. It was so definitive. The huge and bustling industrial port was home to at least two ferry companies and a hovercraft, as well as commercial ships. Before the Channel tunnel between England and France was bored underneath the Straits of Dover, vehicles and their occupants sat in snaking bright lines waiting to load onto the boats. Neatly organized into arrival and hence boarding lanes, you watched the lorries go first and then the bigger vehicles, camper vans full of families going to France for summer holidays, cars and then motorcycles. Everybody going somewhere. Leaving England. Waiting. The huge ship appears and snugs up to her dock. Hawsers lash tight, the gates open, ferry workers bustle around, and the ramp descends with a solid thud to allow the ship to regurgitate her belly full of cargo from twenty miles across the sea. Then it was filled again. The actual Channel crossing took about an hour and a half, but the loading and unloading was a process and sometimes you had to wait for the next boat if the one you were aiming for filled up. Pack your patience and prepare to camp out. The whole experience was a part of the trip at that time; it's probably way more sanitized now. Your vehicle was ushered onto the giant boat in order and by lane. A ferry worker made sure you were as close to the car in front as possible, "Leave 'er in gear, handbrake on!"

The vehicle deck was like a giant cavern, everything painted British Leyland green, the smells of oil and diesel and the clanking of chains against metal grates. The boat creaking against the pier, workers barking orders.

You weren't allowed to stay in your vehicle and climbed the central metal stairway to the upper decks and the 'lounges' with plastic chairs and grubby carpet, a gift shop and a self-service canteen. The canteen was similarly stocked as the British Rail of old and motorway service stations, stale sandwiches with the corners curling up, unidentifiable snacks of one sort or the other, bags of crisps and coffee that looked like weak tea and smelled a bit like coffee. Mars bars were the safest bet and salt and vinegar crisps. The huge cargo doors were slammed shut and the massive hawsers released. The clanking ferry slunk away from the dock, and its human cargo stood on the decks and watched the White Cliffs of Dover disappear. An hour or so later, the Pas de Calais appeared through the sea fret. Disembarking seemed faster. The ship regurgitated its contents onto the wrong side of the road and off we went to foreign climes. The Calais terminus led straight to the open road, unlike in Dover, which was in the middle of the town. It felt alien. A road, wretched refugees from Eastern Europe camped along the sides trying to find a way to England. Chain link fences topped with barbed wire. Not a welcoming place.

Being the last French frontier, Calais and surrounding area had known a lot of gruesomeness in its long history of wars. The town of Dunkerque, where British sailboats had evacuated thousands of English servicemen retreating from the Germans at the end of World War II, is not far away. In the centre of Calais, which I visited once because it occurred to me that I had driven past it a hundred times and never seen it, there is a bronze statue by Rodin titled the 'Burghers of Calais', dedicated to the heroism of six of the city leaders during a siege of the city in 1347. They had eventually surrendered the keys to the city. Naked and in chains with nooses around their necks, they were spared a painful death. It's a strikingly miserable statue. The French specialize in grim and tortured expression, masters of the dramatic pose. That's my only recollection of Calais; it made an impact.

The region known as the Pas de Calais has many memorials to war, none so striking as the endless fields of small white crosses across the countryside in the areas where the battles of the Somme were fought. The English and Allied Forces were driven back to the ocean by the Germans and millions were slaughtered in hand-to-hand combat. Mass graves, no names, memorials in every town from Calais to Rouen and Caen as you head southwest as the crow flies to Spain, avoiding Paris and all the *péages* or toll roads.

I would spend a lot of time in Paris later but for now, expensive cities were not the goal, tourism not the intent. To avoid the *péages* was a bitch though. I swear to this day that the person who invented the French road system was a blind drunk. As you sailed merrily past the exit you needed, the sign just beyond it clearly announced that you were meant to turn there, and the next stop would indeed be the toll booth. Stick to the D roads or Route Nationales, not the faster, more direct A roads or motorways. The long way did make for good adventure, and I would never have visited any of those beautiful country villages if not to avoid paying for tolls AND petrol. The little green camper slowly ate the miles through the French countryside, the cities of Tours and Poitiers to Angoulême and across to the Bay of Biscay and the vineyards of Bordeaux. In other adventures, I would always take different routes through this huge and beautiful country and often went to the northeast of Paris then south to the Mediterranean or west through the mountains to Andorra, the tiny principality nestled high in the mountains on the French border with Spain. Andorra was a tax haven and a good place to buy cigarettes and booze really cheaply, other than that, a half-hour stretch of road. Blink and miss it.

Finally, a new shining sea lay before me and the road wound down through the tourist towns of Bayonne and the world-famous Biarritz to the Spanish border and the port town of San Sebastián, which had been a stronghold on the Spanish border with France for centuries as well as the port town of the Basque nation, Euskadi, or País Vasco in Spanish. Politics in this part of the world in the 1980s were marked by social discontent and violence. The Basque separatists were strong and the signs and graffiti on the roads were all in the Basque language. There were many tiny towns, and all spoke a dialect of the language, sometimes only maybe a thousand people with their own language. The Basque people fought hard to preserve their separate identity and it was wise not to spend too much time in Basque Country. The people were suspicious, their Romany heritage and desire to be left alone, highly apparent.

I stopped for lunch in one roadside town and sat at the bar to eat tapas. The shelves behind the bar were stocked with jars full of strange apparitions, preserved, wrinkled and bizarre. Snakes and eggs and tiny creatures in brown liquid, mixed in with fetal animals and unidentifiable objects. A witch's pantry or a museum of the odd? Who knew. Appetite dulled, I stared a little too long and was hustled out the door. I drove on through Pamplona, city of the running of the bulls and all the miles through Zaragoza to Valencia and the Mediterranean, keen to start my tattooing adventure, but not knowing how it would all play out.

The first official traveling tattoo bus client was to baptize my tattoo station in Alicante.

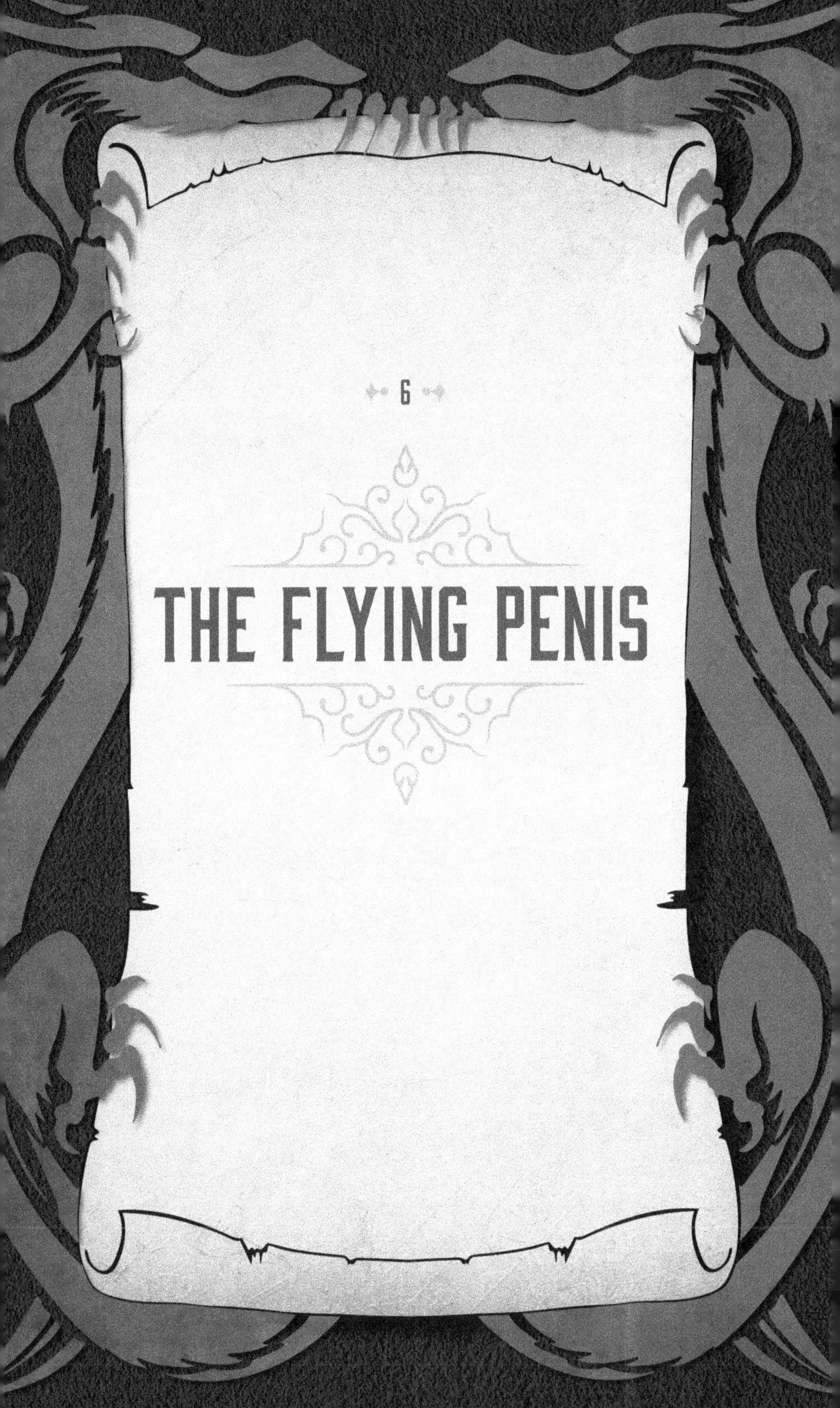

6

THE FLYING PENIS

licante is a city on the Mediterranean Costa Blanca, named for its endless white sand beaches. It has its own medieval fortress and a marble-laid promenade that started within the old town and continued along much of the seafront; the Esplanada de España. Lined with palm trees and market stall vendors, terraces of bars and cafés also run the length of this wide and vibrant walkway. The lifeblood of the city, it's the perfect spot for afternoon strolls and family activities. It was also a huge attraction for street performers in the '80s and in my previous life as a street artist, I had spent many a day there catching coins.

I parked close by and walked up the promenade to see if any of the travelers I knew back then were entertaining the morning crowd. Spain was in clean-up mode at that time though and trying to get rid of a lot of the scruffy foreigners in favor of a more refined look which would, hopefully, attract more Northern European money. The sad part of this endeavor, especially in the Costa del Sol in Andalucia, was that many of the local residents sold their family homes for what was to them a lot of money and found themselves priced out of the real estate market living in nasty crumbling tenement blocks. The stench of bitterness and disgust from the locals was strong for a long time, as the English and Germans settled in to gated communities of opulence, refusing to learn the language and giving very little back to the country where they now resided. But the European Union had yet to sanitize all the charm, and most of Spain was still happily dozing in the Dark Ages.

Very few street performers were about; a couple of travelers lurked by a fountain, huffing on a 'chillum' (carved stone marijuana pipe wrapped in a cloth), their bedrolls and a backpack in a pile. I walked on, refusing the proffered pipe with a smile and a wave. I could hear a strange, unidentifiable jumble of screeching noise and headed in its general direction. The noisemaker came into view. He was a beggar, a Spaniard with long black dirty hair and a lush beard. He had only one arm and no legs. There were many similarly handicapped people in Spain at that time due partly to the Spanish Civil War, which had ended in the last decade with the death of Generalissimo Franco, and also, in greater part, to the way in which the Spanish drove cars, rushing headlong to their death or dismemberment like maniacs at full speed in vehicles with no doors, very little braking capacity and definitely no seatbelts. I saw many horrific accidents and more insane driving in Spain than in any other country until I travelled to Mexico many years later. Most handicapped people did not get any kind of money from the Spanish Government and if they had no family, were highly reliant on the church and soup kitchens and the kindness of the general public.

They also had other hustles to make money, like this particular *caballero.* He had found a tape recorder machine and recorded some very crazy, loud and debilitating noises on it, screeches and howls and crunching mechanical sounds. He would lay the machine on the ground in front of a busy restaurant on the esplanade at lunch hour or evening dinner, press start and yell and scream into an attached microphone. The easiest way for a manager to deal with the aural assault on his patrons was to pay the man to go away. It was a very effective way to make some money and sometimes get some food to go with it. I watched the show and was amused by the theatricals and the innovation. I sat on the terrace and chatted with the man about the town and the day as he got ready to pack up his tools of his trade, folded bills in his grubby hand.

The restaurant manager was bustling around keeping an eye on us and quickly came to ask me if I was going to buy something, so I ordered myself and the beggar a beer. Mine came in a glass but the scowling manager brought a bottle for my new friend and told him to please take it to go. Our brief chat ended. The man chugged the beer down.

"*Gracias señorita! Que tenga un buen día.*"

"*Igualmente!*"

And he shuffled off, using his one hand to move his body, stick supporting the other side. Happy. I sat and watched the people walking and drank my beer. A server came over and wiped my table down, bringing me a menu. At first, I thought it was a man because I could see a beard, but when the person spoke, she had a soft feminine voice. She chuckled and explained that the beard was from hormones from "the Pill' back in the day, and it was easier to leave it longer than to trim and have stubble. She said it amused her to see people's reactions and that she didn't care, and neither did her husband. We chatted about the street life, and it turned out that she was German and was working her way back home. She knew several people in Alicante and would put the word out about my tattooing. I should come back tomorrow.

My first paying customer was there the next day. I remember the actual tattoo that I was asked to cover up really well. It was a hand-poked jailhouse penis with testicles and wings attached. Who knows if it was a drunken event, a bet lost or just funny at the time, but there it was, unmistakable in all it's glory on his right upper arm. The tattoo's owner was a young German guy, kind of goofy and friendly enough, a backpack traveler, dirty and wearing raggedy clothes in the oppressive heat so his body odor was a little overwhelming. He wanted his tattoo covered up and I wanted to do a tattoo, so all the cards were on the table right there and he was a perfect candidate, he just didn't care what he got as long as the penis was gone. He didn't have much money, but he had enough for me to fill my petrol tank. We settled on a design of a naked lady with butterfly wings, definitely a step above my actual skill level as a technical tattooer but I could draw it and my artistic ability carried the day. I had the van parked on the beach where the paved road ended just north of town. It was fairly level and I set out all my tattoo gear. I asked him to leave his stuff outside, the space being small and him being stinky.

Gloves on and go time. I scrubbed his arm with alcohol taking off most of his tan in the area around the tattoo. I drew the butterfly design over the faded hand-poke and made it disappear. The penis tattoo was soon gone, and the butterfly wings were an improvement to the whole. The customer was happy. It would have been cool to have a camera to mark the moment but this was before the age of phones in our pockets or cameras you could throw away. Sadly, I have no photos of this great adventure. I drove back to town and went for a beer on the esplanade to say thank you to my German waitress friend, but she was already gone for the day.

I was excited, my first paying tattoo on foreign soil was in the books. It was time to head further south and towards Gibraltar.

Almería was the next stop on the road to the Rock. It is another city with a huge fortress, reminders of the Arab influence on Spanish lands. Almería is also one of the hottest cities in Europe and had to have its water supply shipped in to its residents at the time. The water was transported on giant rust-bucket tankers that loomed in the bay and the water ran ferrous red out of the faucets. Non potable. Despite that, there was a lot of agriculture in this area, mostly olive tree orchards and in the mountains, *Datura* plant, similar to Jimson weed. There were many stories of people who came to the area just to find the plant and disappeared in the high desert, literally lost on *Datura* weed and its psychological rollercoaster effects.

The day was already very hot, and I decided to keep going. It was a short hop to Almuñecar where I stopped in to visit Pete Bonner, an English tattoo artist who had moved to Spain in the early '80s shortly after the death of Generalissimo Franco. Spain had been isolated from the world economy and endured years of divisive tension during the dictatorship of Franco. People were ridiculously poor and the infrastructure was in tatters at that time. Some rural communities had never seen cars; I encountered that once firsthand about twenty miles out into the *campo* from Gibraltar. The van was surrounded by men with pitchforks as soon as I pulled into a village on a dirt track. They made me turn around and leave. The country had not yet been ordnance surveyed; the maps were pretty sketchy, at best, off the beaten track.

Pete had tattooed by hand in England and continued to do so when he moved to Almuñecar. He then got some rotary machines and began tattooing people in their houses but as he tells it, drunk customers, jailhouse stories and lack of money became too much. He said that in the early days when he first moved to Spain, the Guardia Civil, who were a very hardcore branch of the Spanish police and remnants of Franco's personal Guard, had stopped him with his little bags of powder color for tattoo pigments and detained him, insisting it was all colored heroin. After hours of relentless questioning, they finally let him go but ordered him not to tattoo in Spain. In the '80s, tattoo income needed to be subsidized by other jobs and he had picked grapes in the south of France to get by. Later, he had opened a shop in Almuñecar, but it was a little too far from Málaga and despite being a great artist, it never really took off and he would go to Torremolinos to tattoo at Herman the German's shop when the Navy ships came into Málaga. The Navy kept tattooing alive in a lot of places back then. You could make enough money in a week to pay the bills for a while. Pete didn't see the need for secrets in tattooing though, he thought it was quite stupid, and helped me out a lot in my quest for information. He also gave me two original Dungeons & Dragons art books which I used for reference and tattoo designs for years after. I still have them. I was extremely grateful for his help and friendship.

During the late 1980s when tattooers were just coming to Spain, there were about five shops in the entire country. The Málaga area had a few because of the Navy base at Torremolinos and the busy tourist presence. A female tattoo artist from Amsterdam named Morbella was rumored to be somewhere around there. She had come to Spain to learn to be a *matador* or bullfighter; unfortunately, I never met her. Linda van Woersem, another Dutch tattooer, was married to Crazy Lucas Hendrickx and they worked for Herman the German; she had just started tattooing also. Another Englishman also had a shop there. Later, running into him in Gibraltar, he would offer me an apprenticeship. "Just come on down to Torremolinos. Anytime."

Málaga airport was the destination for holidays to the South of Spain. The city was overbuilt and an oversold mecca of all things vacation, catering mostly to British and Germans because the French had their own Riviera and didn't venture South much. British and German beer, food and flags were everywhere. Potbellied, bright-red holiday makers trying to avoid the locals. Gypsies trying to pick pockets. Junkies trying to get high. Amsterdam of the south. It held no interest for me, and

I kept going through the towns stretching south of Málaga's sprawl; Marbella, playground of the rich and famous, Fuengirola, Torremolinos and a host of other small towns that are probably pretty big cities by now. I remember Mother telling me that Marbella was such a cute fishing village when she had been there in the '60s. I couldn't begin to explain how much it had changed. I'd probably feel the same way now myself.

I reached Gibraltar and went to visit Keith and Steve on the Castle Steps. They were both singularly unimpressed with my idea of tattooing out of my van around Spain. They said I needed to clear it with Mao, who was really the kingpin of Spanish tattooing at that time. He owned a shop in Madrid and another in Rota, the American Naval base by Cádiz. I don't think they thought for one minute that I would make it much past that. I had seen Mao in passing, he was big and scary looking. Not my first rodeo though, so I pointed the van north and headed for Cádiz, wondering why this step didn't apply to Steve's travels.

Rota was a huge base, a stopping point for the American aircraft carriers patrolling around Europe and about as close as the U.S. military could get to the gates of the Mediterranean, 100 km from Gibraltar, although their ships would stop there too. It was extremely neat and clean for a Spanish town, there was a very obvious presence of money in a wretchedly poor country. American dollars were everywhere. Visiting sailors from the aircraft carriers spent their shore leave in similar fashion to those in Gibraltar, consuming huge amounts of booze and getting tattooed. Military personnel were posted to the Rota base year-round, meaning resident customers. The only tattoo shop in town belonged to a Spanish biker, and he didn't tolerate people trying to sneak in and open up on him. I remember Mao being very large and intimidating. Of course, I was small and scrawny, and well aware that he held the key to my being able to travel in his country and tattoo without any problems. I knew who he was and had a lot of respect for him. Years later, after I had established myself as a proper tattooer, we would have a professional relationship and laugh about that meeting in Rota. He was actually a very nice guy.

Business was different back then, though. At first, he laughed and said no when I explained what I wanted to do, along with the proverbial, don't be ridiculous, women don't tattoo. I pushed it. But I have a sterilizer and I make new needles every time. Too dangerous for you, he replied. Well, I'd traveled quite a bit in Spain on foot and was well aware of the dangers; street smarts win every time. Eventually, he agreed to come and take a look at my setup and may even have been slightly impressed by how clean it was although his scowl didn't change, just the flicker of an eyebrow.

"OK," he said, "just make sure and keep it clean or I will call the health department. And don't work around here." I shook his hand, his big bear paw almost crushed mine, but I tried to keep a straight face.

Relief! I couldn't work around Cádiz, but Spain was a big country. There were a handful of other shop owners whose areas I would also avoid. Nobody likes a scratcher.

So now, there was just the small hurdle of trying to hustle up potential clients.

How hard could it be?

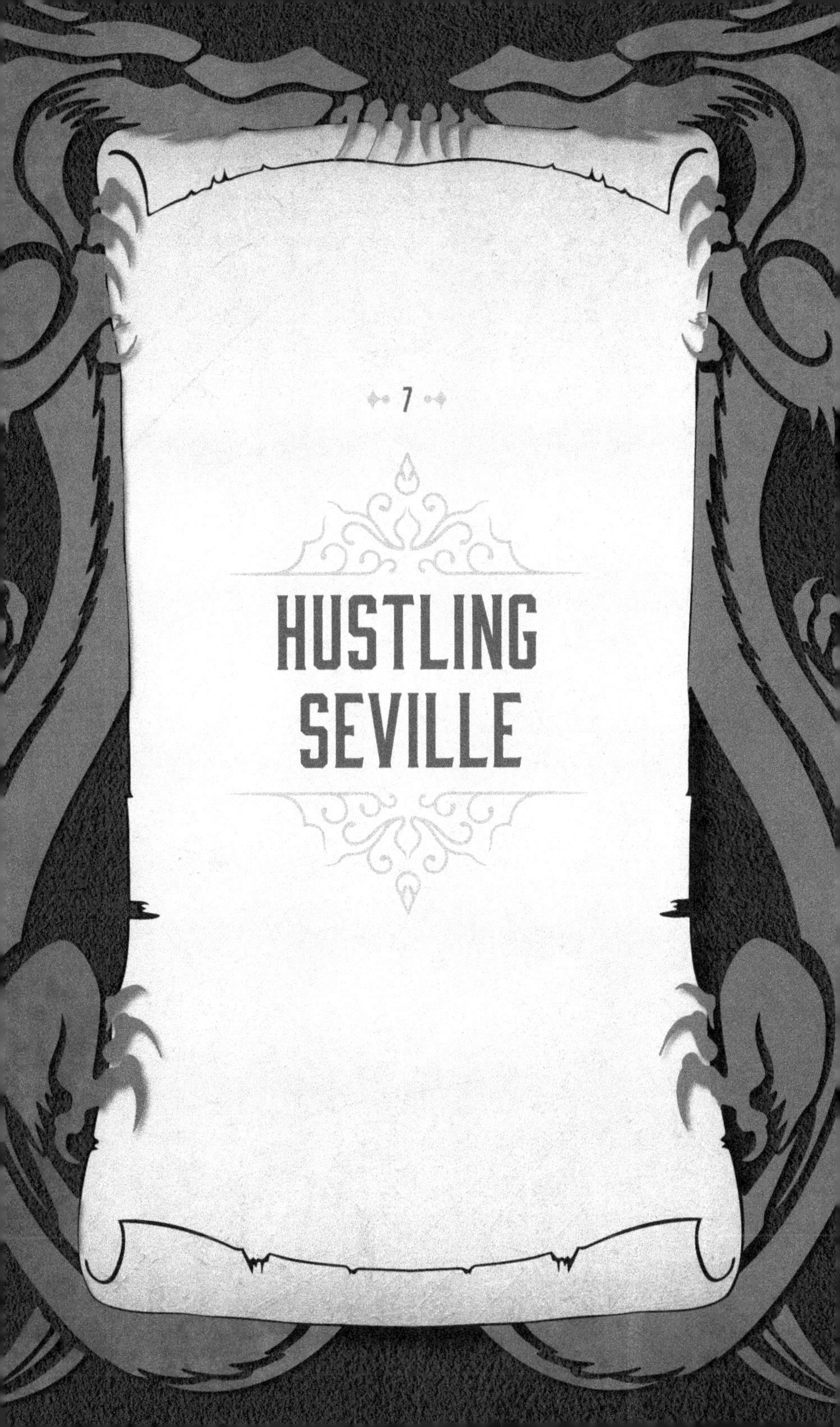

7

HUSTLING SEVILLE

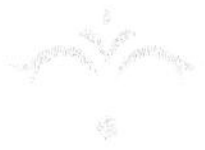

drove the 100 or so miles from Rota to Seville with a practically empty petrol tank. I would need to make some travel money soon, especially since I needed to drive in order to charge my batteries to run my tattoo machines. I was hopeful Seville would bring customers, lots of them.

Seville is one of Spain's oldest cities. It's Moorish fortress, the Alcázar, sits above the Rio Guadalquivir, conjuring up images of conquistadors, galleons and the Spanish Inquisition. It lies about 40 miles inland from the Atlantic coast and the treasure ships would ply back and forth, bringing goods from the newly occupied lands of the Spanish Empire. The battlements of the fortress are the old city walls, with four huge stone gates looming over the entrances to the original core settlement or Old City. Some of the original road still existed, huge flat slabs of red stone made up its surface, no cars allowed. The shadows between the narrow stone buildings were full of dust and busy eyes. There were some seedy businesses and a lot of bodegas inviting the thirsty. At night, the whole place came to life. It was not a safe place to be alone, but it absolutely was where I planned to go and find potential tattoo clients, or so I thought. Networking in bars in England had been a good way of drumming up business.

I spent my day in the huge Parque Maria Luisa, hiding from the heat under the trees, and walked along the banks of the Guadalquivir River, checking out the city. The wide Malecón, or avenue, had lots of seating where people could meet. Elegantly dressed Spanish locals sat and chatted with friends, these people wanted nothing from me. There were plenty of foreign travelers and buskers and street artists. I could make trades with them for tattoos, but they didn't have any spare money. I knew the routine from my days as a street painter. It seemed that finding people to tattoo wouldn't be as easy as I had thought, but the city was bustling with workers, getting everything ready for the upcoming Seville Expo, so I wasn't ready to give up yet.

I was very nervous about leaving my van unprotected because if broken into I would lose everything, including my precious tattoo equipment. I preferred to be in my vehicle after sundown but at some point, I was going to have to leave it if I were to go to the Old City and scout the bodegas. I had spotted a dirt lot edged with trees close to the main road. It was behind the American Embassy building and seemed to be a good spot for one vehicle. Generally, travelers' trucks all parked together but that only meant being moved on frequently, and not all the occupants were above stealing from each other. I inched the van as close to the embassy building wall as I could. It was before the days of vehicles being towed away for no particular reason. I buried my tattoo gear as deep as I could in the well of the battery box under the seating area, locked up and left, nervous.

I slipped into a dimly lit *bodega* in the Old City. It was more open than a British pub, with people sitting around at tables, playing cards or dominos and drinking. I was used to leering men and their ways, I had been around truckers, bikers and bars for long enough. But being a slight blond, white girl in a Mediterranean country was something way outside that realm. It's a fact that Latin men relentlessly hit on light-skinned women with blue eyes whether they were attractive or not, and they weren't subtle about it. I was wearing Doc Marten 18-holer boots, torn pants and had a short mohawk and a few tattoos on my arms. It turned out that I attracted all kinds of attention, but not in the way I had hoped for. All my attempts to talk about tattooing fell on deaf ears.

"Don't be ridiculous, girls don't tattoo," was the only answer I got to all my attempts to sell tattoo work. Some just spat on the floor and walked away, their eyes told me that the fact I had tattoos meant nothing about me knowing anything about the subject; others just continued to hit on me. There were no young people just older men and drunks. There were no women in the bar other than the owner's wife, serving food at the tapa counter. After a short while, which felt like an eternity in real time, she came over and asked if I was a prostitute. I was surprised and answered no. She said, "Well, that's what they think you are, so you should probably leave if you don't want any trouble." I told her why I was there and what I was trying to do; she snorted derisively.

"Don't be ridiculous," she said "women don't do tattoos! Now get out of here before you get yourself hurt!" She spun on her heel and walked off.

I slipped out the side door into the dark alley and walked quickly, staying in what little light there was in the center of the walkway as unseen things skulked in the shadows. My head was spinning, I wondered how I was ever going to make this work. I'd been pretty sure that the bars would have the clients, like they did in England. But this was not England and I felt pretty humbled and dejected. Now what? Spanish machismo for the win? A form lurched from the shadows towards me and snapping out of it, I ran full speed for the stone gate, not waiting to see what it was. This was not the way to go, the bar woman was right about the dangers of wandering the streets at night alone.

The next day, I spent sitting in the parking lot in my van, wondering what to do next. In the afternoon, a man in uniform approached and demanded to know what I was doing there. He was the security guard for the American Embassy. I spun a story about not feeling well and just wanting a rest and he told me to park further away from the building, to which I answered that I felt that it may not be safe left unattended in the middle of the lot if I left to get food. He said he'd keep an eye on it for me, so now I had a security guard but no time to lose.

That evening, I heard rock music coming from somewhere and could see lights in the park on the other side of the big avenue, it looked like a concert. I walked over and there was a metal band playing and lots of young people hanging around drinking. I started talking with some of them. The girls were mildly horrified as only good Catholics can be, but we chatted about tattoos at least and they laughed nervously. Girls, it seemed, didn't get tattooed either. One went over to the group of boys and whispered to her drunk boyfriend, pointing at me and giggling. I felt that at least this crowd was more receptive than the night before, so I hung around and watched the show from the back. A short while later, someone came up and tapped me on the arm and I turned to see the drunk boyfriend. He was quite insistent as only drunks can be that he wanted a reaper tattoo and how much was it. I wouldn't normally have tattooed him as drunk as he was, but he could stand up and talk and I was desperate to tattoo somebody. It was as good an opportunity as I was going to get. A group made its way to the van with me, and I did the reaper tattoo. The guard came over at some point and although he was surprised by the tattooing, he seemed more curious than annoyed. Eventually, the kids left. It was 2 a.m. The next morning, I woke up to the noise of people talking outside and opened the back doors to a small crowd waiting outside the truck wanting tattoos. They had liked the reaper tattoo, the price was right, and the word was out! I tattooed them all, even the security guard.

One of the kids had family in Granada. He told me people were hoping that I would drive there and tattoo them. I did a circuit between the two cities for a couple of months which doubled as a way to charge my batteries and even though I was tattooing slowly and more than carefully in those days, did a lot of work. Being able to practice tattooing and make a little money was great and I was grateful to have found a small customer base. They were thankful for me because the closest tattoo shops were miles away. It worked well for all of us. None of the girls ever did get tattooed.

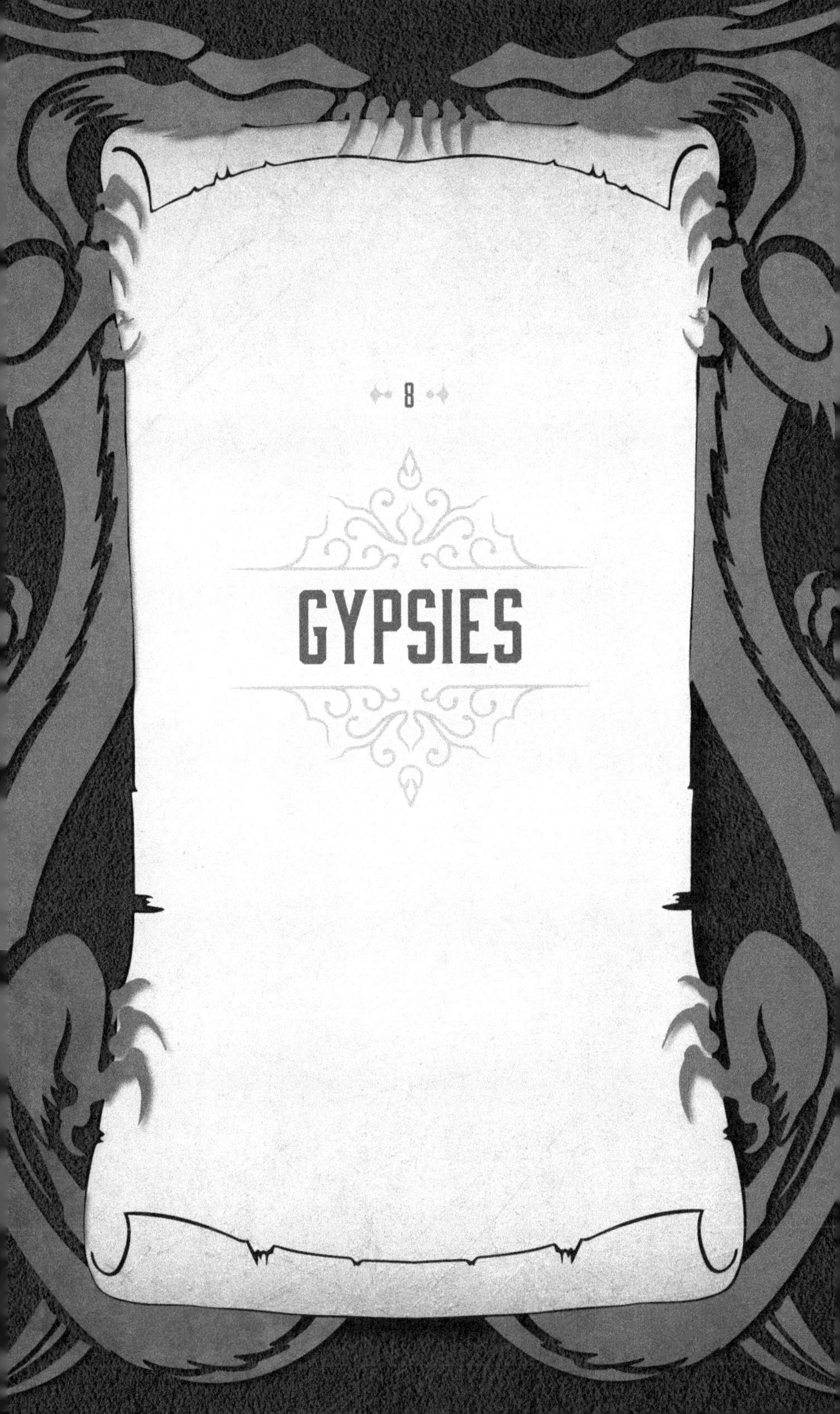

8

GYPSIES

A small grubby child stood in the middle of the dirt lot crying. Huge sobs made her little body shudder and the tears running down her face left streaks as they fell on her dirty dress. I couldn't see anyone else around and so I went to investigate and see if she needed help. Through the blubbering I understood that she had lost her puppy. A woman was heading towards us now, fiery eyes and swinging earrings against her long black hair. She grabbed the child's thin arm and pulled her away, glowering at me and telling me to leave her child alone. I told her that I was just trying to help, and she softened slightly at the sound of Spanish, not English. She told me that the girl's puppy had indeed run away that morning and if I should find it, they were parked on the other side of the Parque Maria Luisa. She described the dog and then scooped up the child and left.

A few hours later, I heard crying noises again. This time it was a small grubby dog sitting under my truck, whining pathetically. I coached it out and gave it a little food and water. It seemed to be in one piece and licked my nose enthusiastically. It also matched the description of the missing gypsy dog and so I walked over to the park to find the little girl.

There were trucks and trailers stacked high with fair equipment and rides pulled off to one side and caravans parked in a circle with a large central area full of chairs and boxes and a fire pit in the center with cooking utensils stacked next to it. I walked into the circle and saw people seeping out of nowhere making a wall through the vehicles, silent and suspicious. This was not good. I put the puppy on the ground. Then a small figure pushed through the crowd and came running towards me and grabbed the puppy in one arm and my legs with the other. The crowd relaxed visibly, some smiled and came forward to thank me, others melted away. There were only women and children there. I chatted for a while and headed back to my truck. Later that evening, I was aware of a lot of commotion and trucks but didn't think much of it. I woke up to the gypsy camp surrounding my little van. I had been adopted. The men didn't speak to me, but all the women now wanted to be friends and feed me, which was welcome. They were curious about tattooing and the noise the machines made; they only knew of hand tattooing methods. As curious as they were, no one asked about getting a tattoo and I didn't push the issue. I still had a fairly steady group of local kids coming by daily. They were a little wary of the Romany people, but it didn't stop them.

The gypsies had arrived in town for the *Féria,* which traveled every year around southern Spain and up the Mediterranean coast to France. It began a week after *Semana Santa* or Holy Week which was coming soon. The *Féria* was a huge event, old carnie style knockdowns and fair rides mixed in with a very Andalucian Spanish flair, flamenco dancing, horses and carriages and *casitas* selling sherry. It would be set up in the huge Los Remedios Park and lay silent until the end of Holy Week, when it was time to start the party. The *Féria* stayed for two weeks in Seville and then would travel from town to the next town, doing the circuit of southern Spain and the south of France where the families would disband for the summer with full pockets. Seville was the season opener.

As it turned out, this was where all the men from the camp were spending their days, constructing the huge carnival rides, hauling massive beams of metal into place, wrenching them all together with enormous bolts and greasing the machinery, checking the soundness of the rides. They were simple. No spinning upside down in cages screaming, just big wheels and rollercoasters and houses of horrors, mild to sort of wild. The sounds of metal being forced to cooperate filled the air for a week and then an eerie quiet. The fairground lay deserted, waiting for its wake-up call. The gypsies partied all day after the work was done and the alcohol flowed. Then came one of the most interesting events of my tattoo career so far.

It was around 2 a.m. and I was sleeping. There was an English girl who had underestimated the difficulty of traveling alone staying with me in the van, sleeping across the front seats. We were woken up by a loud banging on the back doors and a man yelling to open up. I was no stranger to being roused by the cops in the night when being moved on from park-ups and as I struggled to find the right level of awake, I grabbed a large knife from under my bed.

"What do you want? "

"*El Jefe* wants a tattoo."

"Come back tomorrow."

And the sound of laughing.

"You do it now. He wants it now."

This didn't really sound like there were any loopholes to be found. The Gypsy King was apparently not to be denied. This was the first interaction I had had with the men of the camp. I stuffed the knife back in its place and opened the door. Gypsies were masters of the knife fight and had shown several cool guys who liked to sport knives strapped to their legs a thing or two about how to use the weapon.

"Give me ten minutes."

The girl up front was terrified, but she got up and made coffee while I put away my bed which was also the tattoo space. The back doors were open, and two men leaned up against the van, watching me, making sure I wasted no time. It was a bit intense; I hadn't been forced to tattoo on demand before.

I set up my tattoo equipment trying not to show signs of anything from fear to annoyance…and I drank my coffee.

Enter the Gypsy King. He was older and had a heavily scarred face and was very obviously in charge. A large-framed man, he barely fit inside the van. He gave orders to his henchmen, telling them to tell me what he wanted. He refused to talk to me personally as talking to women was below his status. His right-hand man told me to draw a design of a blonde woman with big boobs, just the top half. He leered at the girl who was trying to melt into the front seat in horror and said, "just like that."

"And don't fuck it up!"

I drew the design, and it was approved with a nod and a grunt and then we commenced to do the tattoo with the help of the man telling me where it should be placed and from time to time mentioning that I shouldn't fuck it up, which wasn't helpful.

After what seemed like a really long time, the tattoo was done, and I showed it to *El Jefe* in a hand mirror. He smiled a crooked smile which I didn't expect at all. It was somehow more intimidating than anything else.

"Good!" He said and then slapped me on the arm like a new friend.

"You come traveling with us!" With that he got up and left.

I would travel with the *Féria* all summer and never see the Gypsy King again. His escorts were around though, and they all eventually got tattooed themselves by which point we could laugh about *El Jefe's* drunken demands. I quietly was relieved that he had only wanted a tattoo.

Now that the ice was broken, the men could all get tattooed if they wanted and although they had little money, they traded to fix my van or would bring food or beer. The women never did get tattooed.

Semana Santa or Holy Week is celebrated in Seville more than in any other city in Spain. It's a big deal. Huge statues of the Passion of Christ looking suitably miserable are paraded through the streets in large processions. The spectacle is iconic in its intensity in this supremely Catholic land and lasts for a whole week. The city closes down, and everyone comes to the show which had been going on in some form since the 1500s. The brotherhoods of about 115 churches organize the details, using floats and statues some of which are hundreds of years old, passing the cathedral and through the narrow streets of the old city. All the floats are carried by hand.

Then there are the Nazarenes, the guys that wear the conical white hats which cover their faces and are very reminiscent of the Ku Klux Klan, but worlds apart in views and location. The image is striking, somehow jarred by modern input. A lot like the Tibetan swastika is often mistaken for the Nazi one. These are the penitents, repenting sin without revealing their identity, and that's what the head gear is about. Thousands of them walked in silence through the streets. There are songs and chants and a night of processions from Holy Thursday into Good Friday called the *Madruga*, or devotion of the virgin and this continues until Easter Monday in various forms. Lots of weeping and wailing and religious fervor.

Holy Week and the endless parading came and went. Suddenly the city was silent, and it seemed as if the church bells had either broken from all the work or stopped for a rest. I was tattooing almost every day, and the only real excitement was when I went to swap the battery charging cables to the backup and accidentally hit the metal frame of the battery box with the hot end which literally threw me out of the back of the van. This caused a lot of amusement among the gypsies. Someone put in a switch for me.

My neighbors began to set up for the *Féria*. The grunt work had been done but now the fine tuning began. Thousands of lights were strung throughout the venue and the party tents or *casitas* were set up. More like small houses, these tents were for both private and public use. Each one received a name shield above the entryway. The vendors unloaded. It took almost a full week but finally everything was ready. I was parked at the back of the *Calle del Infierno* behind the rides and concessions. I wasn't on the main drag or even advertised, but I didn't need to be.

Saturday at midnight the fair was lit up, all 60,000 lights of it. People swarmed in through the high and wide brightly illuminated entryway. The sounds of flamenco came from loudspeakers and the *casitas*. There was food and tapas and sherry, lots of sherry. The private tents were for family and friends only, some had the canvas drawn but others watched us watching them and cheered and smiled. High society. Sevillans in full traditional Andalucian dress on horseback, in carriages, on foot. The rides began to turn. The *Féria* was alive!

No one seemed to tire of the fair, it was free to all to enter. The carnies worked tirelessly, and the people just kept coming. For me, I tattooed mostly carnies and that was enough.

The most popular tattoos were religious themed; Jesus and the Virgin and praying hands and so on. I had drawn up a bunch of variations to have them handy. I had made needles til my fingers were so burned on the tips that I couldn't make any more, and everything was ready to go. It was hot in the van. There was a small electric fan and the windows were open but people getting tattooed don't always do well when it's hot and one afternoon, a large pasty man passed out while I was tattooing his arm. In the back of a camper van, the setup is two bench seats across from each other so I would sit on the edge of one seat and have the person I was tattooing turn the body part that we were working on towards me. It was mostly arms and legs, not really possible to tattoo much else due the limitations, so when the man passed out, he fell between these two bench seats....and was stuck. It's probably almost impossible to imagine the scenario but there was a large gentleman stuck, fortunately face up, in my van. When people pass out, there are various things that you can do to wake them up and you should do it as quickly as possible. Anything from buckets of cold water in the face to slapping should do the trick. If you have smelling salts handy and want to be civilized about it that's ok too. Mostly don't let the person swallow their tongue or stay out for too long. Meanwhile, I'm trying to pull this guy up to a seating position and slapping his face to wake him up, no cold water handy. Someone walking by saw what was going on and came in to help me and we managed to get him to sit up. As soon as the man came to properly and assessed his surroundings, he literally ran out of the van and I never saw him again. Hopefully he eventually had his Lord's Prayer tattoo finished.

After two weeks everything ground to a sudden halt, a lot like *Semana Santa*. The fair melted into the night and in the morning, all the parts were gone. The gypsies made to break camp and I wasn't sure where to go next. As the trucks roared to life, *El Jefe's* henchman stopped by to tell me that I was invited to roll with them.

Next stop Ronda....

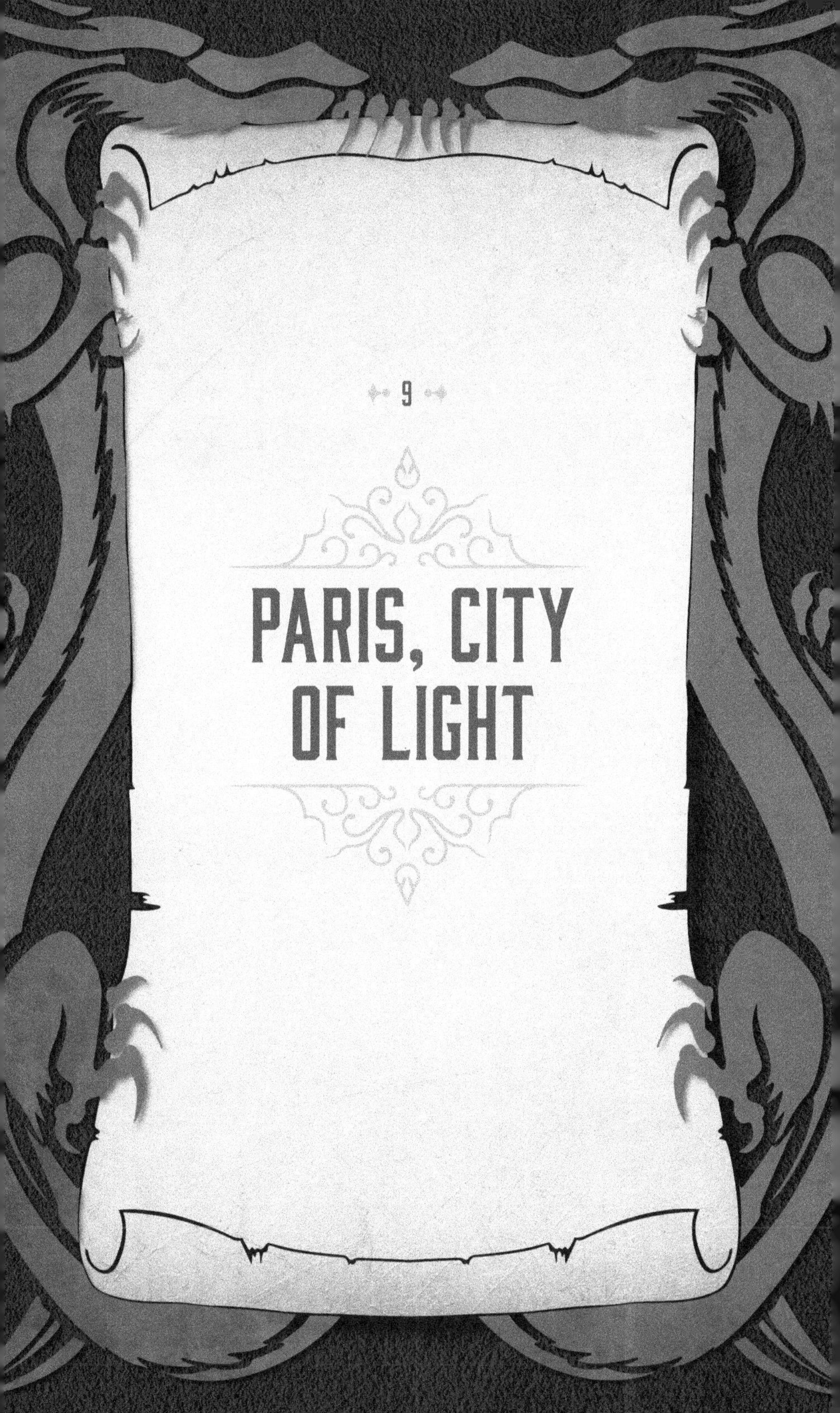
9

PARIS, CITY
OF LIGHT

The lumbering, colorful convoy of trucks and caravans that made up the *Féria* traveled through small towns and large cities in the south of Spain and slowly up the Mediterranean coast to the French Riviera. The booths and rides were set up and broken down, the routine becoming familiar, the clank of machinery fading into background noise. Faces blurred and the excitement of the fair became a normal thing. I parked a little way from the main drag and tattooed a few people, mostly local day workers from the surrounding area who came to make a little money helping with the set up…then spent it. They were excited to find a tattoo artist, we were thin on the ground. When I wasn't working, I wandered among the milling crowds and enjoyed the sounds of the fair, happy people, excited children, the smells of barbecuing meat and cotton candy and sour beer.

Spain at the time was not a clean or necessarily pretty place. There was a lot of poverty and bad sewage. No traffic lights and no real infrastructure as the country struggled to regain its feet after years under the regime of Generalissimo Franco, who had kept Spain in a reign of brutal oppression for almost forty years.

The *Féria* brought fun and excitement and a roaring good time at least for the weekend.

The rich, colonial architecture in cities like Barcelona with its Sagrada Familia cathedral, still unfinished over the centuries, and Avenida de las Ramblas, home to prostitutes and bird sellers, were as visually stimulating to visit as always. There was one tattoo shop in the whole city at that time, tucked away somewhere in the old city by Las Ramblas. I never did manage to find it. Tattoos were still firmly in the realm of 'bad' in this heavily Catholic country. I hustled a lot and did relatively little work, so I used my spare time to tune machines and draw pictures, trying to refine my design skills and fill up my large sketchbook.

My small traveling van had no selection of flash designs other than what I could draw up. I leaned heavily on religious motifs, and they seemed to sell well. I also had my two Dungeons & Dragons books for reference and practiced my hearts and roses with the obligatory banners. I had very little stencil paper to apply the designs to the skin and mostly drew directly onto the skin with a ballpoint pen. I can't really explain how difficult it was at first to focus on the design as well as the techniques of applying the tattoo at the same time. Pen lines disappearing with one misplaced wipe of the sweating client's skin, heart-sinking to watch, and all too common in the summer heat and atrocious lighting. I didn't know then that if you start in the bottom right-hand corner of the design and move from there keeping the palm of your hand away from the design, you run a lot less risk of annihilating your entire drawing. Lessons learned the hard way and a lot of stopping to redraw the pattern.

Everything was trial and error. I came to figure things out as I worked, there being no substitute for the human skin as a medium at that time, and every tattoo became a little better. I tattooed myself. I even tattooed a dead, cold, squishy pig's leg, but only once because it was so gross. Pig skin was fairly close to human skin, but the tactile sensation was definitely off-putting.

In Montpellier, France, the *Féria* disbanded for the rest of the year. They would meet up again in Seville next Easter. As the last gypsy caravan disappeared down the dusty road to rejoin their families, I went to rejoin the traveler community of mostly Germans and English lounging in the South of France.

The Convoy or 'Legions of the Great Unwashed' as we nicknamed them, were around and generally to be avoided as their number was largely made up of drug addicts and thieves, but there were also just people living in their vehicles in any town that would let them stay for a while. There were fairly organized 'park-ups' or groups of mobile 'homes' ranging from small, converted vans to big trucks with boxes on the back and built-out double decker busses. These would usually be in a field on the edge of town and looked a lot like the gypsy camp. People who had traveled together before meeting up somewhere new, some had children and looked for the safety net of like-minded travelers. None of these folks had much money for things like tattoos but I could trade for fuel and food. Things went stale. You can only trade for so much fuel and food.

My desire to do more tattooing was now a driving force that couldn't find a source. I decided to move on from the South of France and tagged along with a French couple that were headed to Paris. They had friends who were living in an apartment building in Montmartre. The base core of the group was family, but they happily and generously shared their space and food with travelers passing through. When we had money, we chipped in. The apartment was huge and there was plenty of space to throw down bedding and sleep. There were artists and writers and students and a lot of connections with street performers and aspiring sellers of art. Quite a few of these were women, the French outlook on feminism being pretty *avant-garde* but not in an overbearing way, women just did their thing, and no one questioned why. Similar to England, except the French girls were more glamorous. The French people have always seemed to be more bohemian in spirit and definitely relentlessly creative in multiple mediums. Art history proves the point, and the architecture backs it up. The Basilique du Sacré Coeur towered on the hill above the apartment, visible from the balcony and a short walk away. Montmartre had been the home of artists since Henri de Toulouse-Lautrec had been making posters for the Moulin Rouge in the 1800s. People painted outside cafes; house fronts were a thing of artisanal beauty, bright flowers spilling from everywhere on the façade.

I spent a lot of time exploring Paris and brushing up my rusty French that I'd learned in school. No one spoke English and it was pointed out often that I wouldn't have made any friends if I hadn't been able to speak the language.

First, I visited the few tattoo shops. Bruno was the old school tattoo master, and a supplier, but he wouldn't let me buy anything and threw me out after I asked. Marcel, who had his own shop but had apprenticed to Bruno, used three different machines to work with, a trait I would pick up later, and he had an extra long clip cord which he passed behind his neck while working so that his hand could better control it. He let me watch for a while. He did very artistic work for the time. Tin-Tin had just recently opened his own shop; he was too busy to be disturbed.

I walked among the art and the history and absorbed as much of it as I could. Statues sprung up around every corner, fountains of bronze and marble in all sizes, stone carvings leering from the high walls keeping the devil at bay. The Louvre Museum was free on Sundays and had no glass pyramid in the courtyard then, although it had been constantly modified since the 1300s. Its buildings glowed with Renaissance superiority. I wandered among the legendary works and was surprised to find out that the Mona Lisa is actually a very tiny painting.

It was a close walk from there to Notre Dame Cathedral where I climbed up to the ramparts and sat with the gargoyles staring out across the city at the Eiffel Tower and the Quais de la Seine where vendors had wooden stands that sold paintings and postcards and magazines. Artists set out easels and painted all day. There were a lot of bookstores to poke around in throughout the Quartier Saint Michel neighborhood, musty pages full of history and that particular smell that only old manuscripts can have. I climbed the Eiffel Tower and stared back at Notre Dame and had the first English speaking conversation I'd had in months with an American tourist who hated French food, which I didn't think was even possible, other than the stinky cheese.

Whiling away the hours sitting outside a *brasserie* with a coffee or beer was the Parisian way to watch the world go by and meet with friends old and new. It was a fascinating city, steeped in history and culture, as were the majority of its residents. The whole city was vibrant and alive.

Raphael Helle came to visit, a photographer who worked in black and white medium only and strolled the streets of Paris every day looking for inspiring raw images of interesting places and people. His work was unique, and he liked to travel around France to find source material for his work. He was heading to Reims to visit some friends who had created and were building a traveling Waltzer ride called *La Chenille* (the caterpillar) that was going to be ready for the local festivals. I tagged along.

The street festivals at that time were filled with true, raw entertainment. Before the days of mass regulation in the interest of protecting people from themselves, an entire local park would transform itself into a mini carnival with entertainers on high wires and trapezes, dancers, acrobats, fire-breathers, jugglers, magicians, tarot readers and rides. A whole world of fun for a week or weekend.

La Chenille came with a big top tent and lots of moving parts. It was based on the popular Waltzer ride from English fairgrounds, similar to the American Tilt-A-Whirl. This fairground attraction had been created by a group of self-styled inventors; welders, mechanics and artists, one of whom was a local tattooer who had a small shop in Reims.

Arno had been teaching himself to tattoo since 1985 and was happy to share ideas and chat about tattooing. He owned the few books available on the subject at the time and it was truly educational and inspiring to be around someone who was driven by the same purpose. He was preparing a French Army radio command truck for tattooing at the festivals. So far, I had only really encountered people who tattooed in smaller vans like my own, so this truck was an amazing beast. It had a toilet and sink and a huge box area which was to be converted to allow two tattooing stations and had a back entrance with steps leading up to it for the customers. Everything was designed perfectly to accommodate the tattoo process. The whole thing was wildly painted in red and black tribal designs including a tent for the entry way and a large tattoo sign.

Did I want to work with him? Did I ever.

I stayed in Northern France for some time, between Paris and hanging out at the shop in Reims where Arno helped me a lot with my quest to learn about tattooing. He had a lot of connections with the art world and knew a lot of the answers to things that I had not yet figured out. He was very open with this knowledge; he knew firsthand how difficult it was to make progress alone. It was odd and yet awesome to have a power pack and electrical outlets. I didn't have to tune my machines to 12 volts anymore but still did, plus the habit of running the machines hot, I couldn't shake. Even with a foot switch, I didn't stop the machine unless laying it down, which used to mean disconnecting the clip cord.

I appreciated it all immensely. He was very much into the tribal style of tattooing, and we spent a lot of time researching that as much as one could with no internet. Arno had quite a lot of customers of his own, enough to pay the bills and his reputation was growing. I did a few tattoos at his shop but there really wasn't much interest in body art in France at that time. The conservative nature of their fashion dictated wanting tattoos like the Mona Lisa the size of a postage stamp, we always joked. Tiny but hyper detailed, practically impossible at that time. I was still thirsty for more work, trying to be patient.

We bought the tattoo magazine, *Easyriders Tattoo* whenever it was available, it was published quarterly, and hungrily devoured it, amazed by the American tattoo world which seemed so much more advanced with their colors and application. I was fascinated by one particular tattoo, an Aries ram head done by Henry Goldfield in San Francisco. It was so clean and perfect. One day while reading the newest edition, I spotted an advertisement by the man who had offered me an apprenticeship that day in Gibraltar. I did a double take. He had a shop in Northern Germany now. Probably not true in retrospect but I felt I could learn more than I was currently absorbing in France, and I had been promised an apprenticeship, which was bigger and better than just practicing, in theory.

Arno agreed that it was a good idea to at least try this new route, adding that I could always come back if things didn't work out. I was eternally grateful to have made an amazing friend in the business and to have met such inspiring people in the local area. I would definitely be back.

I pulled out the Michelin Europe roadmap, dusted it off and looked for Hagen, Germany. Then I went to the phone box, fed some coins into the machine and called the number listed in the magazine. The owner sounded surprised to hear from me but said I could come and work at his shop. Good news. I got into my old van and headed to the German border.

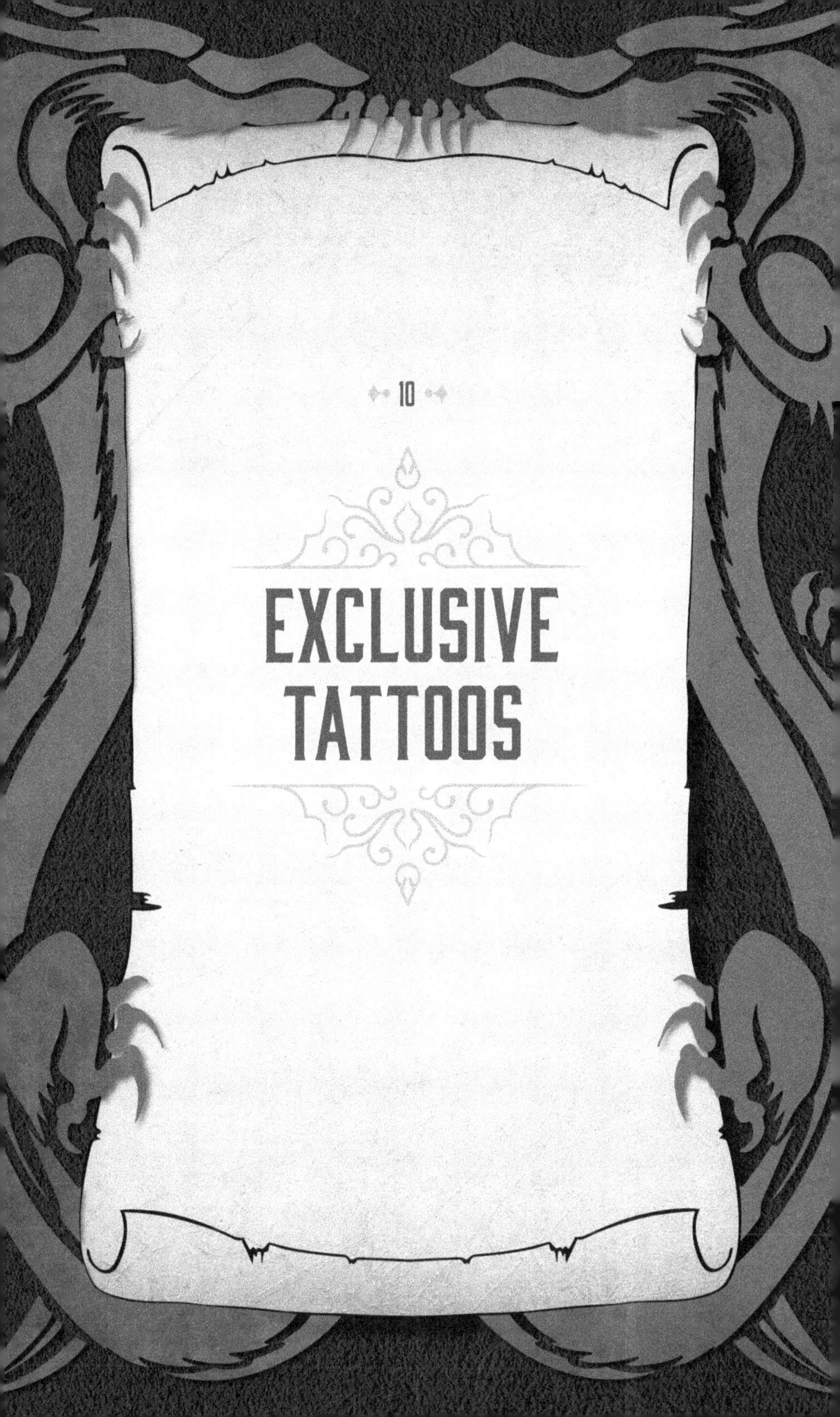

10

EXCLUSIVE TATTOOS

The shop in Hagen was easy to find, there were no other tattoo shops in the town, which was in the middle of the Ruhrpott region, close to an industrial sprawl of other towns and cities. The owner and his teenage son and daughter were welcoming. He had left Spain due to not being able to make enough money to pay the bills, which was pretty common in the days when tattooing was not yet popular. He had also been close to a shop owned by Crazy Lucas, who was a local Spaniard, and they didn't get along.

His shop was pretty basic and not very clean. I was surprised to find his tube and needle set-ups loaded in their machines sitting in disinfectant for days on end because the 'perfect' combo had been found. I had heard about tattooers that did that and would only change needles once a week or when they finally became too blunt to use, but that belonged in the past in the realms of washing down tattoos with a sponge from a communal bucket, didn't it? His regular customers joked about it when they stopped by, asking for appointment times on the days that the needles would be fresh…but they still got tattooed. They didn't seem to care. Mao's insistence on cleanliness and my own desire to be professional kicked in. Was there a sterilizer? I dug it out from under a pile of books and dusted it off. It was a dry heat sterilizer. I half expected there to be a moldy pie in it. I brought my field autoclave in from the van and set it up on my gas burner. Everyone was highly amused.

My new boss asked to see photos of my tattoos. I didn't even own a camera. He explained that there were tattoo walk-in clients in Germany, which meant that people would just come into the shop and ask to be tattooed on the spot, and they would want to see pictures of my work before committing. American service personnel who were used to being tattooed in the States got tattooed here, and there was a big pool of locals to draw from. Tattooing in Germany leaned mostly towards the English and American tattooers that had opened shops there, close to the military bases. Alf Diamond, probably the biggest influence on the German tattoo scene at the time, owned the Frankfurt Tattoo Association, FTA, and was bringing friends and associates over from England to work for him. They in turn would open their own shops. The Germans didn't have much access to equipment and learning but were slowly apprenticing to the American and English tattoo artists and buying their supplies from the States or England. The flood gates were opening. Germany was a fresh young tattoo market, and the work was there for the taking. My boss had heard about it through the tattoo grapevine in England. Older Germans and the bureaucracy weren't very hip to tattooing though and found it all mildly horrifying.

I tattooed the boss's kids to have live evidence of my ability while I bought a camera and tried to build my portfolio a little. There was daily work, and I learned a few things about different needle groups and inks. The owner was a good artist on paper and had a clientele for bigger work, but he wasn't really into being a mentor, and was mostly drunk. He also smoked cigarettes whilst working with dirty gloves on. I used my opportunity to gain experience and make some friends in the local area. I also got to see a lot of the American style of tattooing in real life, not just in magazines. Thick bold lines and brilliant colors. I also now had more time and space to draw designs, and a little money to buy art and tattoo supplies.

The shop's owner was from Yorkshire and friends with Kevin Heath, a tattoo artist from the FTA who had worked in Frankfurt for Alf and then in Karlsruhe for Larry of Larry's Tattoo, an American ex-serviceman. He had been tattooing since the mid '70s and was opening his own shop in Schwäbisch Hall, close to Stuttgart. He was looking for an artist and could I be there for his grand opening, which would be in April '92. He had a strong customer base of his own and was looking for someone to do the smaller stuff and keep the shop open while he was getting things up and running. A closed door has always been just that on any business, even when the sign on the door says, "Back in five minutes." I could also speak German; like French I had learned it at school, which was very helpful in a town further away from the American bases.

Kevin's new shop was named Exclusive Tattoos, which was a major upgrade in a world where Skin Deep, Body Art and

Tattoo (*Easyriders* logo) were the main staples for shop names. I got there before the grand opening to meet my new boss and get used to the new environment. It was classy and clean; Kevin was very motivated to establish a new standard of tattoo shop and he liked to be flashy. It had all the latest available equipment that could be bought and a shiny tile floor and even leather couches. The opening day had over 300 visitors, we made one appointment.

But the shop began to take off and there was a tattoo to do almost every day. Kevin was showing me new things; new needle groups and a different, much easier way to solder them which did not involve using a needle jig and was much faster once I got the hang of it. You couldn't make too many needles; it was always good to practice, and we had plenty on hand. The shop had an electric steam autoclave which made everything more efficient. Kevin's knowledge base of some seventeen years and working with other tattooers was extensive, and he was happy to help me become a better tattoo artist, which was very welcome, and I soaked up as much information as I could. New ways to tune machines, how to trace a proper stencil without too much extraneous crap to confuse you, how to use a stencil machine (new state of the art stuff), how to stretch the skin more easily, the importance of a good light and good photos. All of that information then had to be put to practical experience, solid in skin. My tattooing was finally progressing, and I could see the results. I had advanced faster in a few months with input from people who knew the trade secrets than I had in two years alone trying to figure it all out. And tattooing as an art form was coming out of the Dark Ages and ready to make its impact on society.

Exclusive Tattoos got a booth at the first International Tattoo Convention in Frankfurt, run by Monique's Tattoo. Monique was an artist from New Zealand and had no tattoos herself, saying once in a live TV interview that the reason why was because they hurt. She was a good media representative for the time though, not at all scary…and female.

It was a big promotional opportunity for Kevin's shop, and he had many existing clients in that area of Germany. At the time, every avenue to get out there was acceptable, but none so big as a trade convention. The American magazines would be there and international artists, so a chance to meet old friends and trade ideas as well as buy flash and maybe supplies. Conventions had been growing in popularity in the States for a while and now they were being introduced to Germany. I stayed at the shop to keep the doors open, waiting to hear all about it on Monday. Kevin packed up and left on Thursday but on Friday afternoon called the shop and told me to get over there with my stuff, they were overwhelmed. I was also a bit overwhelmed at the idea of working at such a big show, but never to be outdone, I was there and ready to go later that evening. Crowds of people milled in the spaces between the rows of artist's booths and pushing through them, I finally found Kevin and he sat me down in a corner of the booth and unceremoniously told me to get to work. We tattooed nonstop through the convention hours all three days. Whenever I looked up, someone was leaning in to ask a question about price or availability.

I would finish one tattoo and get ready for the next, there was a wall of faces and ready clients. I didn't have time to fumble or seem unconfident. The convention floor was so busy that it was standing room only. I did more tattoos and made more money that weekend than I had ever dreamed possible. It was exhausting, but exhilarating. In the hotel lobby, I saw some of the big name tattooers I had seen in the American magazines, Kevin introduced me to some of them. I was too nervous to even remember who they were later. Tattooing in Germany was firmly on the international map. It was 1992.

Convention floors are laid out pretty much all the same, from shows that sell Tupperware to tattooing. I remember a convention center that had both those shows on the same weekend which was truly amusing as the frumpy old ladies looked appalled and refused to pass the tattoo artists in the hallways. Needless to say, they didn't get tattooed.

There are booths arranged lengthwise and usually back-to-back facing another row of the same, in a large hall or banquet room at a hotel or exhibition space. The booths display their wares, and the customers can meander and check it all out and talk to the vendors. At a tattoo convention, the tattoo artists in the booths are ready to tattoo and the public can check out who they want to have do their tattoo on site, enticed by the bold banners behind the artists, the selection of available flash, the portfolio of photos of the work they have done. There are competitions every day of the show for different style categories of tattoos and anyone that wants to enter them, and be judged onstage, can. Best of Day as well as Best of Show. The format is still largely the same, but the quality is no longer always there, as people with no interest in the trade other than making money from it, hand out high rent booths like candy to all comers. But in the early days of tattoo shows, all the artists had to send photos of their work to the organizer to be vetted for standard. The organizers were tattoo shop owners and wanted to present good quality, artistic tattooing to the hungry public who ate it up and there was never any shortage of attendees. Photographers did their thing and TV cameras and radio presenters would move through the venue, looking for interviews with the attending artists. It was all fresh and new and exciting.

I had first attended a tattoo convention in Amsterdam at the Paradiso in 1989. The building itself was a night club and had balconies going up around a main floor. It was packed. The legendary American tattoo artist Ed Hardy was there, and I spent most of a day glued in a corner on the outside of his booth, watching him apply a huge Japanese tiger sleeve freehand. I was there so long that he eventually commented on it. I was too awestruck to answer. There was actually a time in my life when I wouldn't talk to just about anyone.

There were many American tattooers there, and some of the more renowned European names. The convention was organized by Hanky Panky, an Amsterdam tattooer with worldwide connections who tattooed American rock bands. It was all very impressive and inspiring.

I hadn't ever thought I would work at one myself. Thanks to Kevin Heath opening that door, I have lost count of how many tattoo conventions I have actually worked at from one end of Europe to North America and everywhere in between. They would become my ticket to traveling the world, I just didn't know that yet.

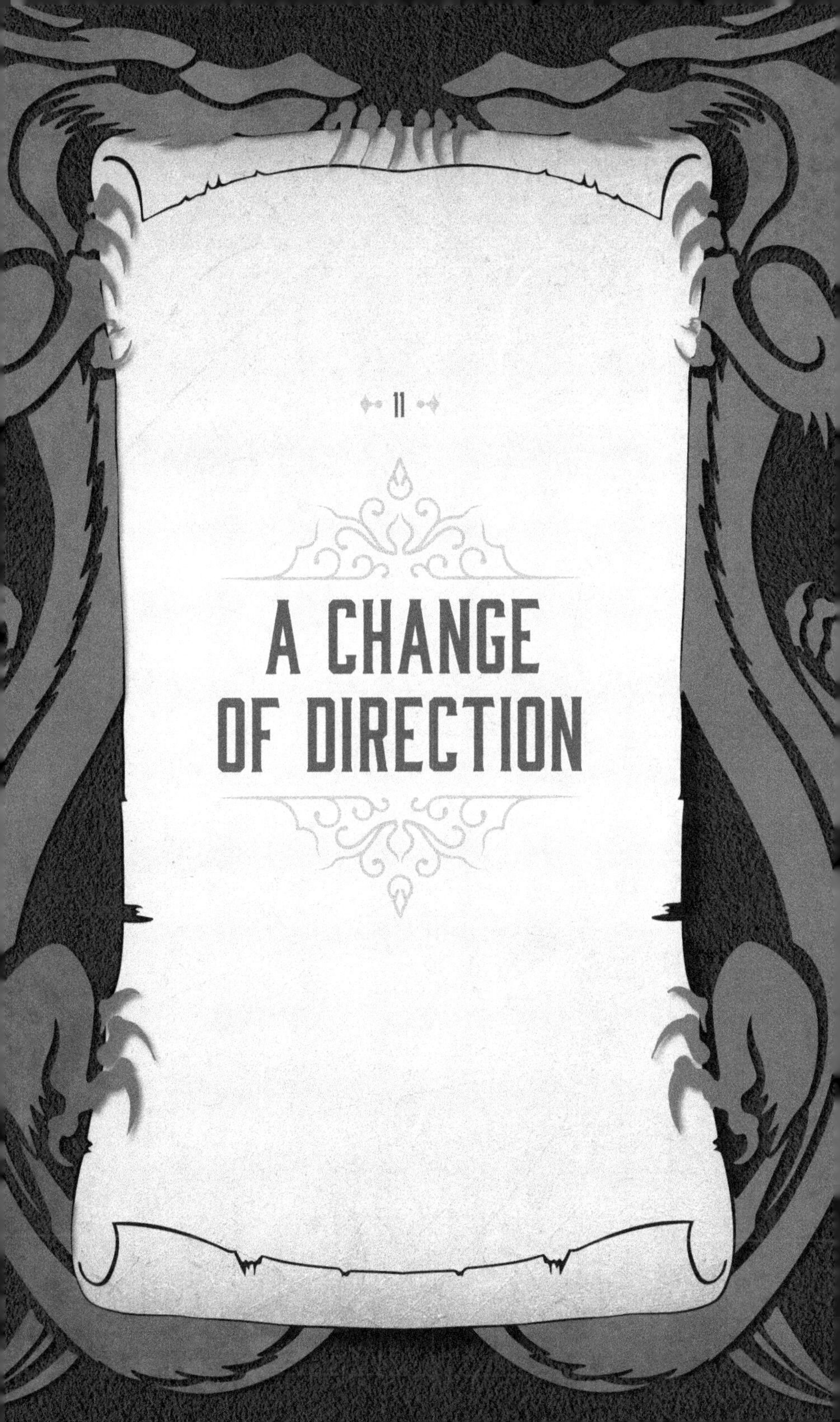
11

A CHANGE
OF DIRECTION

I worked for Kevin for a while longer, ever learning more and enjoying working from the new commercially available flash designs that were starting to become popular, designs from the States and other European artists would arrive in the mail. A set of seven sheets was the standard, anywhere between five and fifteen designs per sheet depending on what would fit onto a 11"x 14" paper, again the standard size. The shop already had designs that Kevin had hand painted over the years but now there were many more styles of tattoo art available.

Larry Kopp was the owner of Larry's Tattoo in Karlsruhe, right next to a huge American military base and he was so busy that he needed an artist badly and asked Kevin if he could spare me, so I went to Karlsruhe with the promise of more work. I wasn't so much hungry for more money as for the opportunity to do more tattooing and learn from different professionals, although more money was nice. Larry also had guest artists coming from England who were popular in the magazines, stars of the day. One was Darren Stares, who specialized in portraits, and I was excited to watch him work. It was a big walk-in shop and had so many flash designs that they were all catalogued and filed in different sizes with the price on each one and the number of the sheet they came from for reference. The sheets were in racks and all over the walls of the low-ceilinged, wood-paneled old workshop-turned-tattoo studio. The shop was dark and would have looked even darker without them. Larry didn't have a photocopy machine to resize the designs as they were very expensive; you had to redraw the design in the right size or walk to the copy shop which took time, and Larry was not big on wasting that kind of time. Redraw by hand we did, and the stencil in its new size was filed for next time, priced and ready to go. Customers would get the same tattoos over and over, the popular motif done just right. I think the one I must have done almost daily during the '90s was what I called "the world's smallest rose," a J.D.Crowe design that I finally timed out at one minute twenty seconds from starting the machine to finish. I have it tattooed on me as a tribute. It's about an inch high with two leaves, a simple stem and five petals, the rose head taking up the top third of an inch. It was the most popular tattoo for women, tucked away on the shoulder or bikini line.

The busiest times were military payday weekends twice a month, standing room only and a line out the door. Larry's was the only game in town and even when new shops began to open, he was the only American veteran so the servicemen favored him. He was also getting ready to open a new shop in a town named Pforzheim, not far away. As the lowest person on the totem pole, I was to go there and keep the doors open.

Larry was extremely paranoid by nature, and he was not easy

to work for. Two people had separate keys for opening and closing the shop, which he always supervised. He was constantly searching the drawers of the workstations for any sign of stealing and checking the money throughout the day. Stencils and tracings had to be cut perfectly to avoid waste. Everything was strictly monitored. I wasn't used to this level of scrutiny and if I hadn't been so busy it would have bothered me more. He had a shop person to deal with the customer's paperwork and dole out the tattoos. Everything was regimented. And there was a contract that each artist had to sign forbidding them to work within 50 miles of Karlsruhe should they quit. These contracts were quite normal in the '90s and were considered binding.

The Pforzheim shop opened and being a brand-new business was very slow. I worked there three days a week. Larry was extremely stressed by its initial inability to make money and took it out on me, accusing me of stealing. Things were not going well, and I had gone from being part of a crew to an army of one. I wasn't sure what to do.

On my day off, I went for a drive out of town to clear my head. Destination Lausanne, Switzerland to visit the famous Leu Family Iron tattoo studio. I had read interviews with both Felix Leu and his son Filip, who was away in the States, rumored to have retired from tattooing at the age of twenty something, having tattooed already for over ten years. He was highly skilled at drawing and applying huge flowing pieces in Japanese-influenced style. He was already burnt out on it all and wanted to concentrate on music for a while. The Leu family were legend in tattooing at that time and the stories of their adventurous traveling life were as loud as the colors in their tattoos. I needed new input, my job in Germany had gone stale. Larry was not interested in helping his artists to learn, we were just there to make money for him. I wanted to go and look at the history on the walls in the Leu's shop and talk to tattoo artists who were passionate about tattooing and its advancement as an artistic medium.

The Leu Family Iron did not disappoint. The studio was a whole floor in their house in Lausanne. There were masks and statues and paintings and photos from all their travels in Asia mixed in amongst huge hand-painted tattoo designs and assorted paraphernalia, hand tattooing implements from the East. There was something to look at in every single space, I had never seen a collection like this, and it was a lot to take in. Felix and Loretta were extremely warm and welcoming people and talked to me about their travels, pointing out photos, discussing the places they had visited and their experiences there. They brought out albums of their work, paintings and tattoos. Books about tattooing from the States, photos of Felix tattooing sitting cross-legged in the dirt in India, things I had never seen or heard of. I wished I had the money to get tattooed, but Felix dismissed this and told me it was simply a pleasure to have a visiting tattoo artist who enjoyed their collection and company. Then it was time for him to work with his appointment for the day, but he told me I was welcome to stay and that someone would be in shortly to answer any further questions that I might still have.

Soon after, a man walked into the room that I immediately recognized from the magazines as Filip Leu. I was thrilled to meet him. He shook my hand as he introduced himself and said that he was home visiting from New York where he was enjoying playing music. He asked me some questions about myself and my tattoo career this far and I told him about my travels and my search for knowledge, a little about those that had helped and those that had not. He began to talk about his tattooing techniques from the layout to the types and groups of needles he used and how to mix grey wash into different shades so that it could be used for large areas and stay consistent. In the days before the supply companies sold premixed grey, this was top secret sought-after information. I was amazed that he would tell me all this, someone he had never met. His answer was simple. If I could and would use the information, that would be a good thing for the advancement of my work and if not, he loved to talk about tattooing anyway. He shrugged it off as nothing, I meanwhile was in complete awe that an artist of his caliber would so freely share his knowledge in simple conversation.

Filip was widely known as a master of large-scale tattooing; I had admired his work in the magazines for years. Despite being nervous in his presence and not very confident in my skill level, I asked his opinion on how to learn more about the artistic application of large-scale tattoos. In a money-hungry Germany where all the tattooers were churning out small flash tattoos as fast as they could, there was little interest in the bigger projects. Our conversation turned to the convention scene and that it was now possible to find guest spots in tattoo studios which were focussing more on artistic style and that every shop owner needs someone to do the little tattoos in the back room while the higher-level artists work up front. The advantage to this would be being able to watch and ask questions and absorb as much information as possible. Progress was within my reach, I just had to find the path to it, and be prepared to travel overseas. North America was where it was happening.

It was probably the most inspiring conversation I have ever had. I rode the high of the massive potential these new ideas promised all the way back to Germany. His words played over and over in my mind. Go to the shows and talk to the North Americans, ask for guest spots. Travel further and learn more.

Nobody was very interested in my trip to Lausanne back at Larry's. I didn't tell them about the things I had learned but mixed up some black ink and water in the amounts that I had been told to make three bottles of grey wash, light, medium and dark. I experimented with soldering some bigger magnum needles but had no tubes that they fit into yet and was scolded for wasting needles. At that time, the shop would supply the loose needles for use. I started to lay out bigger designs and was teased relentlessly for it.

A well-known English tattoo artist came to the shop for a guest spot. He did bright color work and free-handed Japanese style designs. I watched him work. There were not many clients for the bigger tattoos and so I asked him to tattoo me, intrigued to watch how he applied the color to get it so bright and solid in the skin. I knew this would be helpful to me, and if you paid for a tattoo, you could even ask questions. The artist was quite high and mighty and was very dismissive of us flash applicators. He put a large lotus flower in black water on my forearm, with a light transparency running through the wind bars and across the center of the flower. This was a new artistic idea that hadn't really been seen before. Artists that saw it later copied it. It took five hours and was a beautiful tattoo. I paid and thanked him. The next day we would finish the dragon that was an unfinished outline on my other shoulder.

I was renting a room from Larry at the new shop in Pforzheim, and the guest artist accommodation was there too. Larry took the guest to dinner and then dropped him off. I showed him his room and the kitchen and then went to go to bed. As I walked down the hallway, I heard him tell me that I could give him his "tip" now. I stiffened, I knew exactly what he meant and up to this point in my tattoo career, I hadn't encountered anything as upfront as this. I was holding true to my determination not to sleep with any of these tattoo artists and suffer the consequences later.

"Fuck you," I replied. "I am not on the entertainment menu," and slammed my door, locking it behind me.

He stood at my door and had plenty to say, acting insulted, as if no one ever turned him down. I didn't say anything about it to anyone 'til very much later not wanting to embarrass him, but it didn't matter. My dragon tattoo from him the next day was the most painful experience he could make it, which is possible by running the tattoo machines really high. I wouldn't give him the satisfaction of quitting halfway through. I was learning a lot more from him than just tattoo technique.

I rented an apartment the next day, very close to the new shop and moved into it immediately. The next international tattoo convention was a few months away, so I decided I would stay at least until then.

A couple of weeks later, I noticed that Larry was monitoring my movements outside of work because I was no longer within the confines of the shop world. One Sunday, his car pulled up in front of my apartment three times during the afternoon and he sat there and stared at the windows for a while each time. The next day, my personal effects packed, I went to the shop at opening time, packed up my tattoo equipment and art supplies and quit.

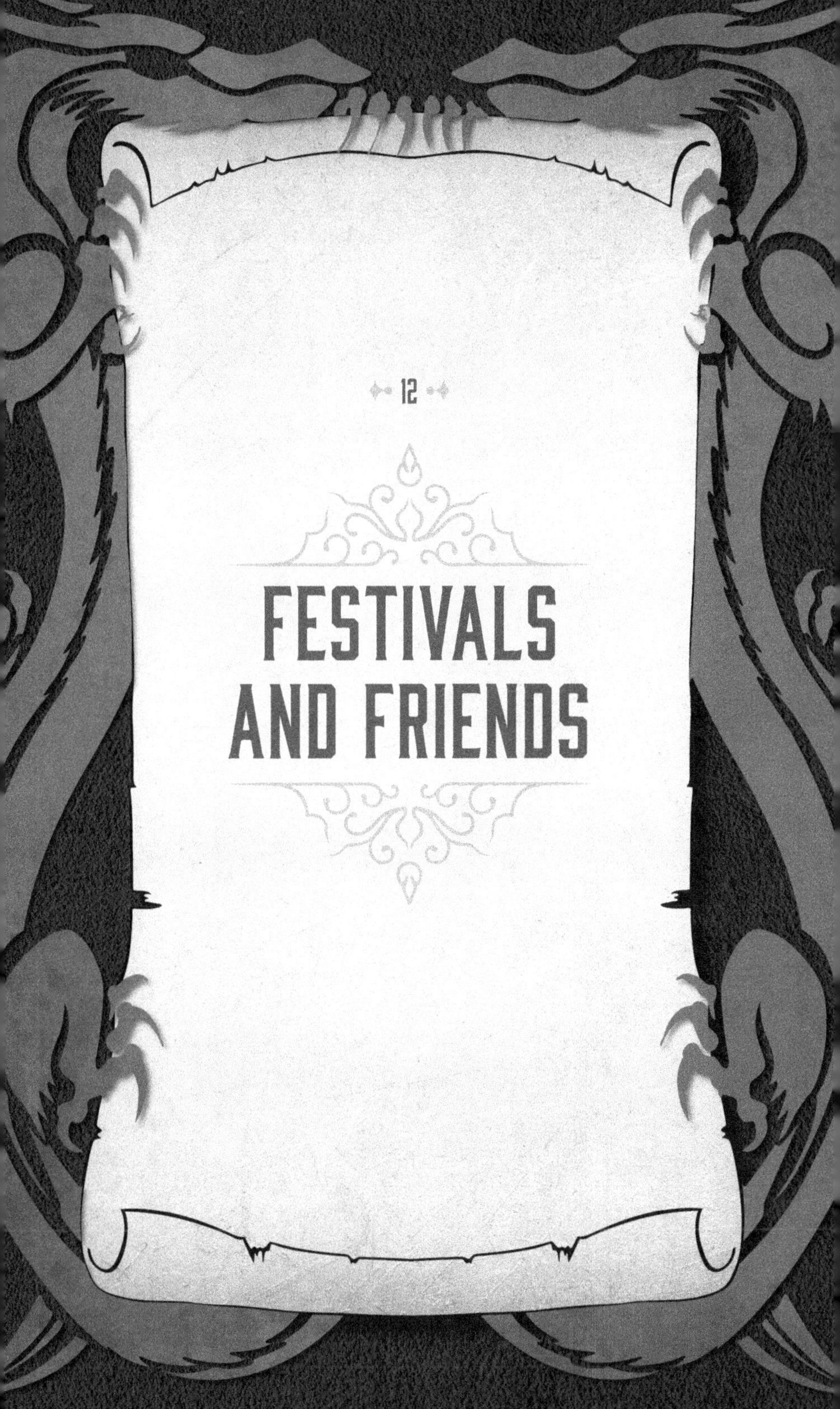

12

FESTIVALS
AND FRIENDS

decided to take a break from working in tattoo shops until the Dortmund international Convention and visited friends that I had made in the Schwäbisch Hall area. Dirk was trying to teach himself to tattoo and while I was not in a position to be a teacher, I knew more than he did and I helped him tune his machines and continued working on his dragon sleeve that we had started earlier. His girlfriend was a good airbrush artist and also interested in tattooing. How they had acquired their equipment, I wasn't sure, but there were definitely ways to do that now outside of the well guarded professional tattoo community. There was quite a bit of underground tattooing beginning to pop up, most of it not very good, but my friends wanted to learn, unlike a lot of what we called 'scratchers' and I remembered Filip Leu's comments. These people were definitely trying to go places so I felt they may as well have some solid knowledge. Never forget where you came from! I knew firsthand how hard it was to beat down the walls of the castle.

From there I drove to France and Arno had finished his traveling truck build and was ready for the upcoming Festival de la Sainte Anne if I would like to work with him there. The little Waltzer ride was also ready for its debut and the creators of all this were currently working on a huge metal dragon for the front of the tarot reader's gypsy caravan. The level of workmanship was impressive, copper sheets cut and fired to change their hue and formed to shape the upper neck and head onto a steel base. It would breathe fire too, a propane line fitted up the structure and out of its mouth. With no email or other visual way of contact than sending photos, it was cool to see all the progress made on these projects in the time I had been gone and be a part of the group of artisans and their bohemian vibe again.

It was refreshing after the stuffiness of Germany where there were relatively few talented creative people thinking outside the box at that time. I was excited to tell Arno about all the things I had learned and share tips and stories about it all, he was impressed by how far I had come in a short time and happy to hear all about it. I also tattooed a couple of bigger pieces, one on a friend from Paris. A large red dragon wrapping her shoulder. Another, a large chameleon winding around an arm in black and grey. My technique was improving, and I was definitely learning more about how to lay out tattoos using the whole body as a canvas.

Waiting for the Festival, I drove up to England to visit friends from my Gibraltar days. Unfortunately, English customs got a little too excited about my tattoo equipment, which was quite common back in the day. There was the comment about women not being tattooists, which I hadn't heard in a while and they tipped all my color bottles out, insisting that I was probably hiding drugs under the color. I couldn't persuade them not to and just like that, my precious colors were all gone. Europe still had borders between the countries with checkpoints, but so far none had been as thorough or obnoxious as Her Majesty's Customs. It would be several years before any of the borders were used to seeing tattoo equipment and they could and did make life difficult, especially at the land crossing posts. Any arguing just meant extra, fabricated delays. I was gutted.

Nick was still in the British Army but had opened a tattoo shop in Dover, ready for his upcoming military discharge. He had been practicing a lot since his apprenticeship with Steve in Gibraltar and was surprised to see that I was still in the game, and we traded tattoos on each other and talked about our experiences. It was a time when tattooists would happily sit and share their knowledge. I told him about my scheme to try for guest spots and he was as unsure about my likely success as I was but mentioned that if he needed help at his shop, he would be in touch. He also had extra color that I bought from him and spare bottles so that if the same thing happened again with the Customs, I could pour the liquid bottle to bottle for the arshole's satisfaction, instead of watching them pour it down the sink. Adaptation. Going through Customs back to France was a breeze, of course, and thankfully all my equipment made it back to Reims in one piece. It was Festival time!

We loaded up the tattoo gear into Arno's mobile studio, it really was amazingly well set up; everything had its place and there was running water in the sink and a working toilet. The electrical outlets all would work once hooked up to AC power and the whole vibe was very professional. Two fully operational tattoo stations gleamed and large chairs for the customers sat on the checkered tile floor. The customer waiting area, stocked with design books was small but efficient and the overflow could wait outside if there was any. No real way to know how it would go but we had more than enough newly made needles and sterilized tubes, just in case. There was a large wooden tattoo sign to go above the entryway tent, painted carnie style, bright and vibrant. There was even a neon sign that went by the steps leading up to the back door where the customers would come in. It made my little van look pathetic in comparison. I was proud to be a part of this whole adventure.

Arno disappeared to help assemble the fairground ride shortly after we had arrived and set up the truck in its assigned spot in the large park. I wandered around and watched all the hustle and bustle as the various vendors and attractions arrived and began to get ready for show time. French street festivals were fairly commonplace, but the Sainte Anne was one of the largest in the area, a three-day weekend that would start at dusk on Friday. It was no *Féria* but there was a little bit of everything with acrobats and artisans and a few small rides, and of course food.

Finally, everybody was ready and as night fell, lights began to blaze, the tarot reader's dragon blew fire, and the people came. The buzz and true atmosphere of Carnival. Arno and I proceeded to tattoo for 18 hours straight. The day acts came in the night and got tattooed. These acrobats were forerunners of the Cirque de Soleil, which was barely an idea at that time, a school for performing arts in a tent in a parking lot in

Montreal! I tattooed a trapeze artist's lower back and was struck with how tough the skin was where she bent backwards over the bar during her act.

The festival was crowded all weekend and then on Sunday afternoon, just as it had arrived, it was gone. *La Chenille* had performed faultlessly, lines of people waiting to ride the little machine as it clanked around its red striped tent. Our tarot reader friend had been extremely busy, and his dragon had been a huge hit. Everybody was tired but happy and our pockets were full of hard-earned money.

The convention visit that I had been building up to was just around the corner and so I headed for Northern Germany. If you're reading this anywhere other than Europe, bear in mind that nowhere is that far away compared to other countries; in the end I could drive all over Europe without a roadmap, that's when I knew I had outgrown it. I left my tattoo equipment with Arno to avoid a Customs disaster, traveling light. It felt weird to leave it, but I was on an official mission to meet and greet not tattoo. I took my portfolio.

The Dortmund tattoo show had a lot of tattoo artists from overseas, mostly England and North America, but also other European countries. A lot of these faces and names were becoming familiar through the tattoo magazines. I wandered through the booths, looking at the portfolios carefully, scouring them for tips and tricks and new ideas. No longer having to beg for information was a game changer, I could actually talk the talk now and was able to share my burning desire to know more about the techniques of the trade. It was an incredible time for the growth of tattooing, and this was a great place to make connections so I steeled my nerves and started to introduce myself to anybody who would pay attention.

I started with shop owners in Germany and was surprised to get a couple of positive reactions to my request for a guest spot. I went with my lifelong theory of the worst they can say is no and it worked quite well. I also now had a shop for a reference, of course, and that went a long way. There was a time when it was impossible to get a chair in a tattoo shop without the owner calling your previous employer. Feeling brave, I approached the most intimidating looking biker in sight, Crazy Ace, owner of Way Cool Tattoos in Toronto and after introducing myself, took the plunge; did he ever bring in guest artists, even ones that were only qualified for the small stuff? He asked for my book of photos and flicked quickly through the first few pages and then, to my surprise, he answered sure no problem, get yourself to Toronto and I'll pick you up. He gave me his card and told me to call him in a week or so once he was home. It had almost been too easy. I wiped the nervous sweat away and decided to take this invitation and not really bother anybody else. I wasn't ready for a no. I'd start with the offer in hand.

Over the weekend, I wandered around at the show and scrutinized booths and books and drooled over tattoo supplies and flash for sale, wishing I could buy something. I needed to save for a plane ticket to Canada now. There were many vendor booths at the show too and I poked around in those. One of them was from a town near Karlsruhe, selling Native American jewelry and leather clothing. Native American art was becoming very popular in Germany, we had recently been doing quite a lot of stylized tattoos of feathers, bear claws, medicine and war shields. I chatted with the woman, and in conversation, she told me that they also had a tattoo studio in their town but were in need of a better artist. I mentioned my contract with Larry, but she said it didn't mean anything. I felt to the contrary, especially since I had pretty much burned the bridge with him just recently and told her I would pass. She gave me a card in case I changed my mind. I said I would pay them a visit if I was headed that way.

The show was over quickly and boosted by my success from heeding Filip Leu's suggestion, I headed back to France and the first available travel agent who could book me a flight to Toronto.

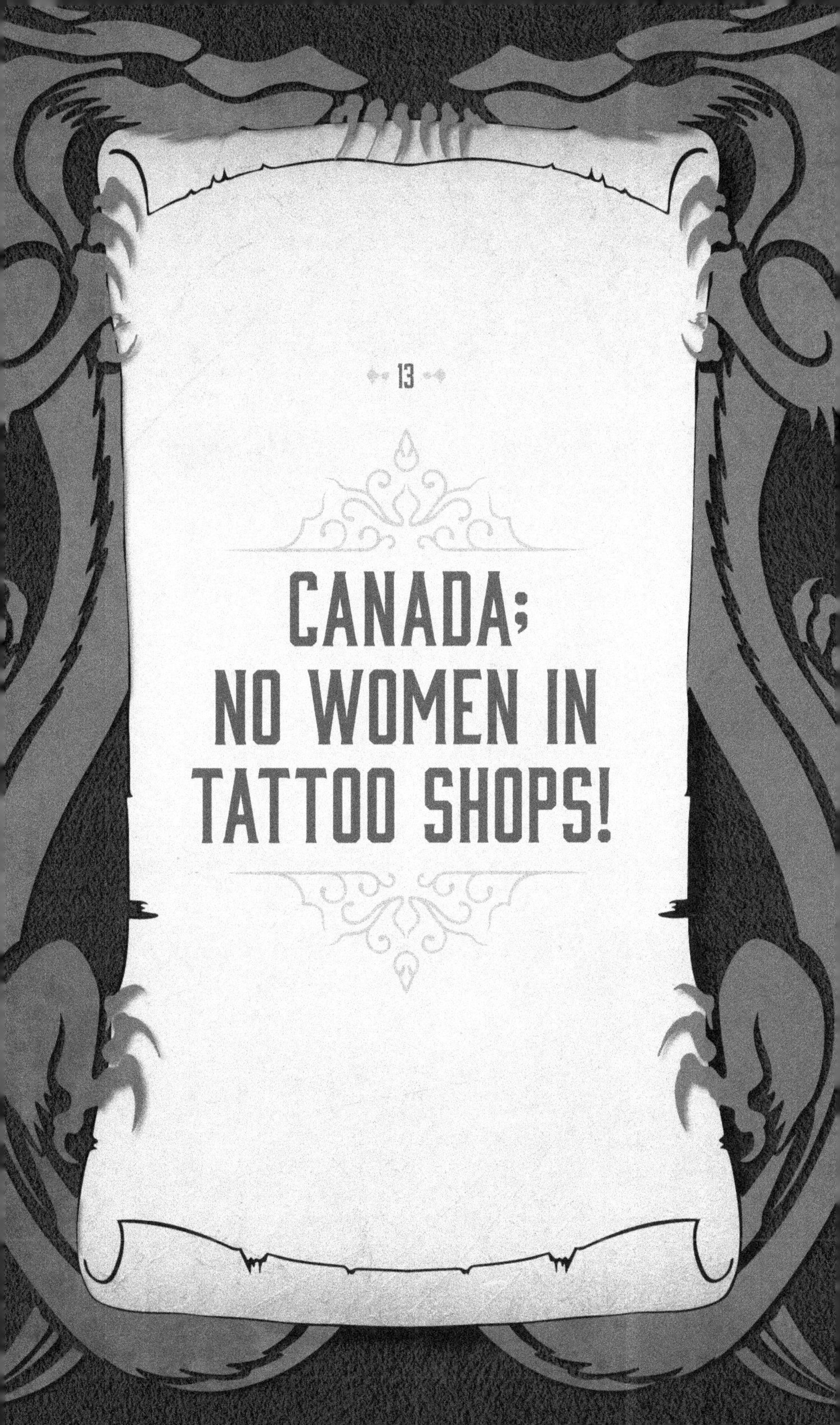

CANADA; NO WOMEN IN TATTOO SHOPS!

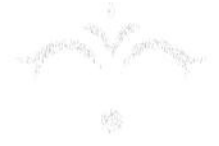

Worldwide travel was the realm of travel agents in their shiny offices full of brochures and posters of white sandy beaches and umbrella drinks, luring us with their promise of the exotic. Toronto was not very exotic, but I quickly had an airplane ticket in hand for two weeks out. My British passport would work just fine for Canada, no need of any special tourist visa or tropical vaccines. I was incredibly excited to go overseas, even, as someone pointed out, if the Toronto tattoo shop owner had not been serious about his offer of work, I could still add a stamp to my passport and collect a new country. I called Ace as promised and he said he would be at the airport to meet my flight and take me to his shop in Niagara Falls to work for a few weeks. We would see how it went and then I could spend some time at the Toronto location if I was a good fit.

I flew into Toronto peering out of the small window at the huge roads and North American semi-trucks. There were six-lane highways and huge buildings in the sprawling city, bigger than anywhere I had ever been. Toronto International Airport was massive and it took me a while to find my new boss even though he towered above most of the bustling people with his tattoos and long white hair. Mostly they gave him a wide berth. Bikers were bad news. We drove for what seemed like a long time during which Ace grilled me about myself and my experience in tattooing this far, and told me he was from Thunder Bay, Ontario, about a 14-hour drive across the Trans Canada Highway. He had recently come back from Indiana with a trailer and his dog whom I would meet if I came to Toronto. He didn't go into why he had left the States but laughed when I asked if he was going back. His Way Cool tattoo shops in Canada were doing well, no need. We pulled into Niagara Falls past tourist businesses offering everything from weddings to viewing live mermaids; it was so different to anything I had ever seen. Culture shock. He left me at the tattoo studio with his manager Harley Charlie who seemed disgruntled. Charlie showed me my workstation in the shop and where the supplies were and gave me my schedule. I could sleep on the couch in the back, I'd find blankets somewhere. It was past closing time. He fired up his big black Harley and peeled out, roaring off down the street.

The next morning Charlie told me that Niagara Falls was his franchise and I had been dumped on him, some chick out of Europe, he wasn't very happy about it, and he'd been told in no uncertain terms to keep his hands off me. I went to work and stayed out of his way. Eventually we would get along well, but I first had to prove that I could perform like a tattooer and do my work properly because, he stated, women didn't belong in tattoo shops. It was the first time any tattooer had actually said this to me since I had started working in shops. Apparently, many American old school tattooers were firmly entrenched in this opinion. From my point of view, it was time to change that by earning their respect. I had faced off with tougher crowds. Besides, tattooing wasn't like breaking rocks in the hot sun for a living, why wouldn't women be able to do it?

Cleaning was a huge deal. Crazy Ace was famously known to turn up at any time, pull on a white silk glove and run his fingers over the surfaces, above the mirrors and frames, in the cupboards, anywhere hard to get to, and if he found any trace of dirt or dust, everyone working that shift would be given a week off to think about it, regardless of status. I cleaned like never before, dusting the museum pieces in their glass cases like a fiend and paying attention to all the details. There were many museums among the tourist attractions in Niagara Falls, and Ace had a fine collection from his years in the States and attending conventions, presents from friends, things he had bought. A tattoo museum contains anything from the early days of tattooing from machines to flash, and curios from old shops. There were shrunken Borneo heads and hand tattooing artifacts from Asia, skulls and old biker stuff too.

Later, I would work at a couple of other tattoo studios with museums, one of which is Triangle Tattoo & Museum located in Fort Bragg, California founded in 1986 and curated by Mr G and Madame Chinchilla. Photos of tattooed people adorn the walls up the flight of steps to the museum. There are a couple of dedicated rooms and items spill out around the entire shop as the collection grows. There is also a sizable display from the old sideshow days. Madame Chinchilla has published several books, among them, *Electric Tattooing by Women 1900-2003.* Each artist featured gave a personal statement about tattooing underneath their photograph. She has three other publications about tattooing, *Stewed, Screwed and Tattooed, Electric Tattooing by Men 1900-2004,* and another on the life of Captain Don Leslie, sword-swallower of Barnum and Bailey Circus fame. The museum's display cases are filled with a world history of everything tattoo and includes my favorite sign painted by Captain Don, who was a prolific carnie painter and tattoo artist, which reads; "To call one's Mother a Whore is a lesser Crime than to call the Sacred Insturment of Tattooing a Gun!" Yes, there's a spelling mistake. Tattooers and carnies famously can't spell.

The tattoo museum in Niagara Falls was next door to the tattoo shop and had a lot of traffic in this tourist town where people famously ran off to to get married in those days. We did a lot of heart tattoos and names. Charlie eventually warmed up when he saw I could handle the walk-in traffic easily and do a decent tattoo. I also cleaned all the dirty equipment and sterilized it for him and made his needles. I only asked questions if I had to, and I favored the position of asking permission not forgiveness. On my days off, I wandered the town and the curiosity shops, Ripley's Believe It or Not!, Louis Tussaud's Wax Works and, of course, I took a boat out to the falls and learned about the crazy people that rolled over them in barrels.

Finally, Charlie was satisfied that I had what it took to go to Toronto and not make him and his recommendation look stupid to the boss. Ace was a gentle giant for the most part but had a temper that would make a person wish they were rather anywhere else, even if they weren't in the direct line of fire. He believed that a person was only as good as their word, and Charlie giving his word for me meant I had better not screw up. Way Cool Queen Street was a busy 24-hour shop with a big crew. Fools were not tolerated.

Ace came down and picked me up, I could work in Toronto for a month, he had a new guy starting then. He told me it was important to always push myself to be better and never to think I was the best I could be because then I may as well just quit. I would always be only as good as my last tattoo. Wise words.

Until I found a room to rent at a house nearby, I stayed on the couch in his apartment, and quietly sat with his giant black Newfoundland dog and watched the comings and goings. Ace was always very courteous and respectful to me, despite the parade of fancy women that came and went. I saw the famed temper a few times in the shop, but it was never directed at me, despite having to take a week off "to think about it" when the white glove came out and there was dust on the top of the doorframe. All tattoo payments were collected at the front desk, and I was paid by check once a week. It was important to keep my paperwork straight to avoid being shorted…no paperwork, no money. I only made that mistake once. I was honestly grateful to not be responsible for the money, I thought maybe Larry in Germany could use that tip. There were at least ten artists, all men, and two shifts. The shop was close to the downtown and the University on Queen Street. The crew got along because if they didn't, someone was getting fired. Ace lived upstairs and could see through walls it seemed. I kept pretty much to myself but joined in the tattoo shop banter and teasing, giving it back as good as I got. It was lighthearted and no one got offended. Shops without banter didn't feel right. Way Cool's Toronto location was exactly what Charlie had said it would be, the quality of tattooing was good but there were no big shot artists doing amazing things out front. I didn't have much free time but did some of the obligatory tourism in Toronto, like the CNE, Canada's biggest annual fair. It felt odd to be a visitor at a fair. I was too tired to visit other tattoo shops.

The girl I rented my room from had some hippy friends who owned a bus and wanted to go to Montreal but spoke no French. They were worried because all the road signs in Québec were in French. I said I could go when my month was up, and Ace called his friend Keith Stewart in Montreal to get me a guest spot at his shop.

Crazy Ace Daniels was a character larger than life, wild tales followed him everywhere, most of them true. He was a showman, a womanizer, a modern-day pirate and a biker to the core. He was tall and large and had a wild look to him with his tattoos and long hair. He was always fair and a man of his word to a fault. Even though his luck in the States had run out, and the legends of his time with Roy Boy Cooper in the Badlands were whispered everywhere he went, he never talked about any of it and moved forward, forging his path across the tattoo trade with a purpose and an incredibly impressive emphasis on hygiene. I would visit with him at conventions in Europe later down the road. I think he had the most influence on me of anyone I ever met, his respect was a huge gift and he had allowed me the chance to earn it from across the world, not knowing anything about me. He later told me he didn't actually believe I would show up; most people didn't. Still, he had given me a place to work and lay my head, even if women had no place in tattoo shops. (His ex-wife Lady was a tattoo artist also.) He passed away in 2010. I will never forget him and my time at Way Cool, which was indeed Way Cool. The world needs more Aces.

On the road to Montreal, I taught the bus dwellers enough French language road signs to get by. They dropped me off and I went to meet my new boss.

Tatouage Artistique was on Ontario Street in Montreal, and there were several other tattoo shops on the same main drag. Normally, a big city might have two or three shops in the metropolitan area, large towns had one, small towns none. Territory was tightly guarded, and restrictive work contracts like Larry's were commonplace. The stories of new businesses on the block, or even too close in the same city, being burned down shortly after opening were all true; rogue tattooers were often beaten, or had their hands broken, their equipment possessed. North American tattooing was the undisputed territory of motorcycle clubs and bikers, although times were definitely changing. There had been some of that in Europe but not as much. You either worked for an existing business or moved on. This street full of competition was something I had not yet seen.

Keith Stewart was not a biker; he was a retired fireman. He tattooed exclusively with a single needle, even the colors and the larger pieces. He worked incredibly fast due to his many years in the trade. Speed came with confidence and a never-ending stream of customers. I had never seen work like that before. He gave me a station in the back of the shop next to Pierre Chapelan, a youngster from France. I don't think he was even twenty years old. His parents had a large tattoo shop in Bordeaux. The rookies belonged in the back room. Out front, there was Keith, right next to the waiting area and then there was a second space occupied by Bill Baker and Scott McEwan at the time, both high level big shot tattoo artists. This was what I had come to find, although at first neither of them was in the mood to indulge my questions or even watchful eye. Keith laughed about this when I mentioned it and told me that to be considered a proper tattooer, I needed to have 100 tubes and then they might talk to me. By the time I left Canada I had the required amount, and the guys were talking to me.

The shop building had rooms upstairs for traveling artists and I spent my days in Montreal tattooing, sleeping or drawing. No tourism. Learning to tattoo well was obsessive. It was nice to have someone at the shop who was also on a quest for knowledge and Pierre and I would exchange ideas and talk about tattooing for hours. I didn't leave the shop much at all. Speaking French came in handy in Québec and I would even translate for the frustrated English speakers in stores who couldn't make it past the storekeeper's refusal to speak English (even though they could), which was pretty common.

Scott was working on getting a full Japanese style bodysuit from Eddy Deutsche, one of the up-and-coming tattooers out of California. I got to watch a part of one session. He was also drawing and tattooing in this new style. Bill, who was from Vancouver and had worked for Paul Jeffries, a famous Canadian tattoo artist from Calgary, was keeping pace and the two of them were doing amazing things. They were experimenting with new needle groups for larger work, which meant tuning the machines to run faster for longer lines and push the bigger needle groups for the color, different machines for large-scale soft shading and color. I was excited to watch it all develop. This was the missing link I had been looking for. I had always thought that tattooing could be so much more, a whole body as a canvas. Repetitive flash was good practice and paid the bills, but it was always somehow lacking to me.

The movement towards bigger and better tattooing was born in San Francisco, home to Don Ed Hardy, who had an extensive background in the Japanese style of tattooing, having forged the bridge from America to Japan years ago. He was very influential in turning American tattooing into an art form from its roots in basic imagery primarily through his contact with Sailor Jerry in Honolulu and subsequent time spent tattooing in Japan. Norman 'Jerry' Collins put tattooing on the map with the American military and along with inventing the color purple, was a formidable master of his time, his bright, bold flash inspiring the standards of the day. Navy servicemen deployed all over the American coasts carried his work, which was then admired and copied in the big port city tattoo shops on the mainland. From San Diego to Seattle and as far as Norfolk, Virginia, tattoo studios knew of him, and some tattooists traveled to Hawaii to work in his shop. They brought home Jerry's spit shade painting techniques for the brightly colored flash and shared their knowl-edge. Spit shade doesn't really involve spit, just licking the excess water from the brush when shading out the ink.

Travel and letters were the prime ways to exchange this kind of information and the connections took a lot of effort. Jerry hated the Japanese for what they had done at Pearl Harbor and could never separate the people and the art from this horrific military event, but he couldn't help but be amazed by their tattoo culture and history, despite wanting nothing to do with them. There is a book of the written exchanges between Sailor Jerry and Ed Hardy called *Sailor Jerry Collins: American Tattoo Master,* published by Hardy Marks; it is a fascinating read. Hardy went to Japan to work alongside the masters of tattooing there. When he came back, he was producing breathtaking, huge tattoos, the like of which had never been seen in America before. Tattooing as a large-scale aesthetic art form had come West. Ed Hardy opened Tattoo City in 1986, hiring Eddy Deutsche, Dan Higgs and Freddy Corbin. It became a powerhouse of tattooing in the '90s. 'Junii' Junko Shimada, a Japanese female tattoo artist who had a full bodysuit, rare for a Japanese woman even now, attended an American tattoo convention in 1987 and met her husband-to-be Bill Salmon. Together they opened the Diamond Club in San Francisco in 1991, welcoming guest artists from Japan as well as Filip Leu. These people were all pioneers of modern tattooing who brought about massive change in the business and pushed for a better standard. There is a term, "standing on the shoulders of giants," which my generation of tattooers really believe in. These artists were among the giants of their time and it's a shame that the respect for what they did seems to be lost. No longer would the repetitive small tattoos without backgrounds be the only available choice, and the budding convention scene was a stimulating way to connect like-minded artists all over the world. Copying became creating.

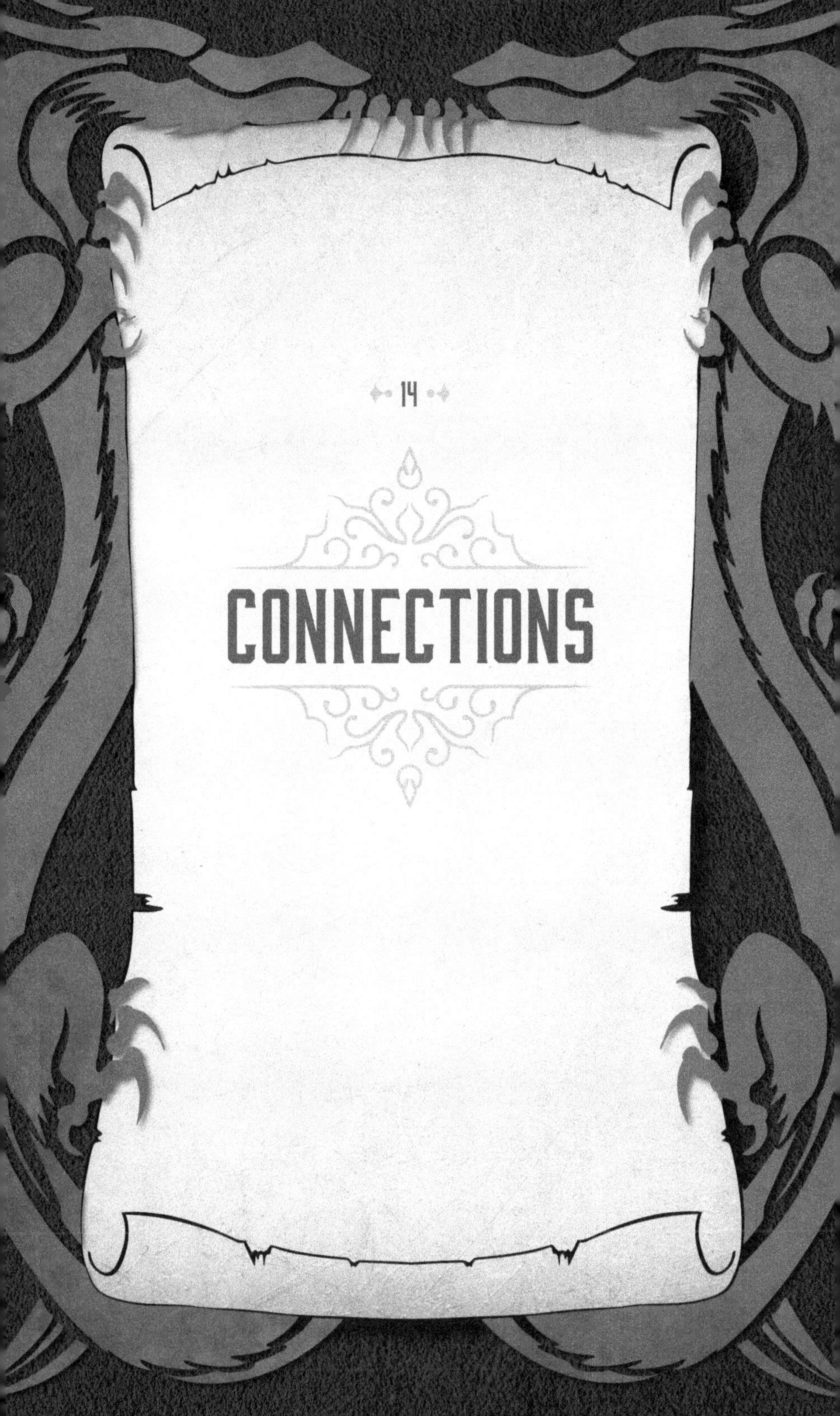

CONNECTIONS

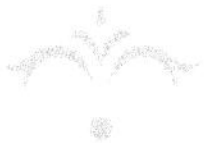

t was truly an inspiring time to be a part of this transition of the tattoo trade. Most people attracted to it now were obsessed with combining and finding the newest techniques to make their own original art stand out from the rest. It was pushing far from any boundary ever previously set, striving to be bigger, better and more appealing as art. I was more than on board with these ideas. We began to look at the human body and all of its curves as an entire canvas, not just parts to slap a stencil onto. The movement of the various joints and the muscle forms could make a tattoo breathe or fly or seem to jump from the skin like the Japanese dragons that were a popular subject. According to Japanese legend a dragon would come alive and destroy its surroundings if it received its eyes before the body was completed, so I always added the eyes last. Colors and background all had a meaning in the Samurai tradition. Water and fire or wind bars and clouds swirled behind and through the main theme.

Bill Baker insisted that drawing Japanese water was the hardest of them all, you had to be careful not to make it look like milk.

He was right. We sketched during the slow times and compared ideas. Bill was testing the prototype needles for his new supply company called Eikon Device, I was happy to be a guinea pig and he tattooed a large carp on my leg, swimming up a waterfall. The water definitely did not look like milk. We used colors from an up-and-coming English supply company, owned by a man named Mickey Sharpz. He also built machines. They were lightweight and much smaller than most of the available American ones, although that was also changing. Information was coming in steadily from people who had met, and worked with, artists from other parts of North America and overseas. Keith Stewart, owner of Tatouage Artistique, would be hosting a large international convention in Montreal later in the year with Dan Allaston from New Moon Tattoo in Ottawa. It was in its second year and a lot of big names were going to be there. The convention circuit was the new information superhighway for us all and it was expanding fast. It was also a great way to open doors across the planet.

I had read about the upcoming Tattoo Tour convention in San Diego and took a week off work to attend it. I had never been to the States, and California was like a Hollywood movie from start to finish. In the airport lines, women discussed boob jobs and the best plastic surgeons. The O.J. Simpson trial was on every TV screen. The Tattoo Tour had a lot of tattoo collectors with huge pieces walking the showroom floor; cartoons and fantasy designs climbing arms and legs, a huge bio-mechanical back piece by Guy Aitchison from Chicago. Paul Booth from New York was tattooing an entire head with a black and grey demon. Dave

Gibson and Eric Maaske showed off their strong American Traditional styles. The Rubbermaids, two women dressed in sexy devil and angel outfits, flounced around serving drinks to the artists.

There were a couple of female tattoo artists that I remember seeing at the San Diego show; Patty Kelley and Juli Moon, but they were so busy I couldn't get their attention. Women took tattooing as art very seriously, no gimmicks or revealing clothing and, strikingly, not a lot of tattoos. I remember that Titine Leu and myself were the only girls with full sleeves on the convention circuit in Europe for quite a while. Not that being heavily tattooed has any bearing on your skill level, it just seemed curious and probably had more to do with the stupid insulting comments that we would get from the general public than anything else.

There was a Japanese artist practicing Tebori or hand poke, I don't remember who. The Samoan tatau master, Sulu'ape Paulo was hand tapping there also, cross-legged on a bamboo mat with his skin stretchers. I was fascinated. The island tattooers seemed just as bewildered by us as we were by them. Their newly revived traditional tattoo culture was an impressive thing to see. There was a lot to look at, all kinds of different tattoo styles I was not at all familiar with and I tried to absorb it all. I had always understood that being a tattoo artist meant you did what the customer wanted, and it would be good to offer them more choices. Specializing in only one particular type of art was relatively new and a train gaining momentum.

Lyle Tuttle was giving a machine building seminar which I attended and was curious to find that I didn't learn much. I had assumed there was so much more to actually learn, but a machine of any kind can only have so many working parts. Tuning them is mastered by experience and knowing what you are trying to achieve. Practice would be the real teacher. Dave Long's seminar about power packs was more interesting to me and I bought a small one which worked on both 110 and 220 volts and could be used in Europe and the States. It was much smaller than the standard-sized monsters I was familiar with and would be great for travel. It still works.

Photographers for the magazines prowled around the show, freelancers like Bill DeMichele, who published the book *The Illustrated Woman,* and Richard Todd, a freelancer, looking for tattoos to shoot. I was featured in the *International Tattoo* magazine edition of the Show, but when told to apply make-up and take all my clothes off by the *Easyriders Tattoo* photographer, I refused, and was told to leave the photography room. Most magazines featured a naked female on the cover with one tiny tattoo, so they weren't quite sure what to do with me in my jeans and T-shirt.

It was a lot to digest, and I was happy to find a couple of Englishmen tucked in a corner, who literally spoke my language and were just as overwhelmed by it all as I was.

Tony Bennett had a supply business on the Isle of Wight in England and was scoping out the American scene. He was there with Paul Sayce, tattoo historian. We went to the bar and in typical English style, they complained about the food and the TV monopoly of the O.J. Simpson trial. Then someone had the bright idea of going to Tijuana, Mexico and drinking tequila.

In proper tourist style, we dutifully got shitfaced and wobbled back to O.J., still on TV, early in the morning. I always forget about the British sense of humor when I'm away from it for a while, and it was a weekend with lots of laughs and piss-taking of the Yanks. I took Tony's card and promised to be in touch. He would be doing the German shows with the English old-timer Ron Ackers and his good mate, Chris Cougar…and of course, selling supplies.

Back in Montreal, it was time to get ready for that city's convention and I was Keith's gopher. I shuttled international tattoo artists from the airport to their hotel, ran errands across town, gathered things for the show and helped set up, all in his fancy Jaguar. Keith's trademark was cars and outrageous suits, as well as a big, matted, single, grey dreadlock that clung to the back of his head, which he refused to cut off despite relentless teasing. He didn't give a shit what anyone thought, and people still talk about it to this day whenever he comes up in conversation. He sat me in his station to work as the big names from around the world rolled in. Everyone was meeting and chatting in the back of the shop. They all stopped and watched me for a minute; it was nerve wracking. A couple of them commented that they were surprised to see me still tattooing, and so far from home, remembering me from Germany or having kicked me out of their shops for asking questions. Not many women really made it far on their own in the trade back then. I was secretly smug.

Show time came and there was one empty single booth, someone hadn't been able to make it. The boss told me to get over there and work if I wanted to, empty booths looked bad on the convention floor. I struggled to maintain composure and happily gathered my gear and some books from the shop and ran over to set up. Opportunity had knocked again; I wasn't going to turn it down. I made a lot of introductions over the weekend especially among the European artists, because I was heading back soon, and spent time chatting with Tin-Tin, the Parisian tattooer who was gaining notoriety in the magazines. His work really inspired me, I eventually would have my back piece done by him. I also met Thomas Lockhart, owner of West Coast Tattoo, Canada's oldest continually operated tattoo studio. I would later work for him in Vancouver and do the National Tattoo Association's conventions in the States with him. He had many fascinating travel stories and a collection of tattoos from Ed Hardy, Greg Irons and the Japanese master Horiyoshi III among others, all neatly capped in three-quarter length sleeves.

Many new names and faces, they seemed to take me seriously too. We were in the business of asking and answering questions, trying to ride the wave of the advancement of artistic tattooing for the benefit of all. It was work hard, party hard and everyone was bonded by a common theme. Tattoo artist arrogance and rock star cliques were still in the future.

A few weeks later, I rode a stretched American limo to the airport, just for fun. Kevin Heath had recently called to tell me that Larry Kopp had passed away in Karlsruhe. My work exclusion contract with him was now void and I would be able to go and check out that shop in Neustadt. But first to the Netherlands and a run to Denmark for the Copenhagen Tattoo

Convention with one of my newly made acquaintances from Montreal, Rob Deut. Rob would go on to become completely immersed in tribal South Seas style tattooing and an expert at it, but in 1994 he was still a rowdy biker. We drove to Denmark from his small shop in IJmuiden with his friend in an LPG-powered car. We spent a weekend being glum with absolutely zero clients, and then the car ran out of liquified petroleum gas on the way home in the middle of the night in the middle of nowhere Belgium. It was definitely a crash after the highs of the recent year, but also a reminder that tattooing was still not viewed well by the public in some places. Routinely, random strangers would make shitty comments about my tattoos and appearance in the street; there were very few heavily tattooed women around, and it just wasn't 'becoming' in their opinion. I was called 'unladylike' and 'vulgar', but I didn't give a crap. My tattoos were my best advertising. Non-tattooed people who apply tattoos always seemed like charlatans to me; if you were going to apply permanent marks onto other people, I felt you should have a few yourself. Just because we tattooers were excited about it, didn't mean the public was though.

I did manage to find a little icing for the cake in that Rob dropped me at Tattoo Peter in Amsterdam, opened in 1955 and the oldest shop in Holland. I got to work there with Peter's son Eddie Wertwijn for a few weeks. History oozed from the walls and the building was in a cobblestone street on the very edge of the famous Red Light District, which was an entertaining place to go and people watch. Hanky Panky Tattoo was across the canal and down aways in a cellar below the Other Place coffee shop. Tattoo stories filled the days, and we laughed at the biker security throwing horrified men back into the rooms behind the infamous Red Light windows. There were a lot of Thai ladyboys working that neighborhood. The punters didn't get to not pay up on grounds of false advertising.

On the way to Neustadt, I stopped at Ralf's Fine Line Tattooing in Düsseldorf and did a guest spot. It was my birthday and I went out with friends to a local bar where I encountered the *Kuemmerlingkreis*. A shot of *Kuemmerling*, which tastes a lot like cough medicine and is way worse than Jaegermeister, came in a small bottle with square slanting sides. Sixty-four of them made a *Kreis* or circle. Making the circle paid 100 Deutsche Mark, and of course I had to show them what I was made of. I showed up to work horribly hungover the next day, to my embarrassment. Ralf laughed at me and told me to go sleep it off, but not before he did me a birthday tattoo.

It was good to work in so many different places and experience each individual owner's approaches to the daily running of tattoo shops. I needed to find a shop of my own soon and put all this acquired knowledge to a daily routine and returning clients. The only test of a good tattoo is how it heals and holds in the skin over time. You have no way to assess that if you are always on the move. Plus, traveling is tiring, and couches are not always comfy; don't let anyone tell you otherwise.

The shop in Neustadt was named Indian Spirit Tattoo and barer and blander than any I had seen. The person hired to tattoo didn't even merit the title tattooer. He was way out of his depth, very dirty, a total scratcher, and the shop had no clientele.

I didn't want any involvement with it. If it had a new name and new ownership, maybe it would have a chance. It was already set up with washable floors and running water and a bathroom. The biggest challenge, the landlord, obviously didn't care that he was renting it as a tattoo studio. That would be the biggest hurdle for years to come as far as finding locations for a business. I told the owner what I thought about it, and that I would pay her to leave the contents and transfer it to me. She said she would be in touch. She was obviously surprised that I was unimpressed, but by then I knew what a real tattoo shop should look like…and this wasn't it.

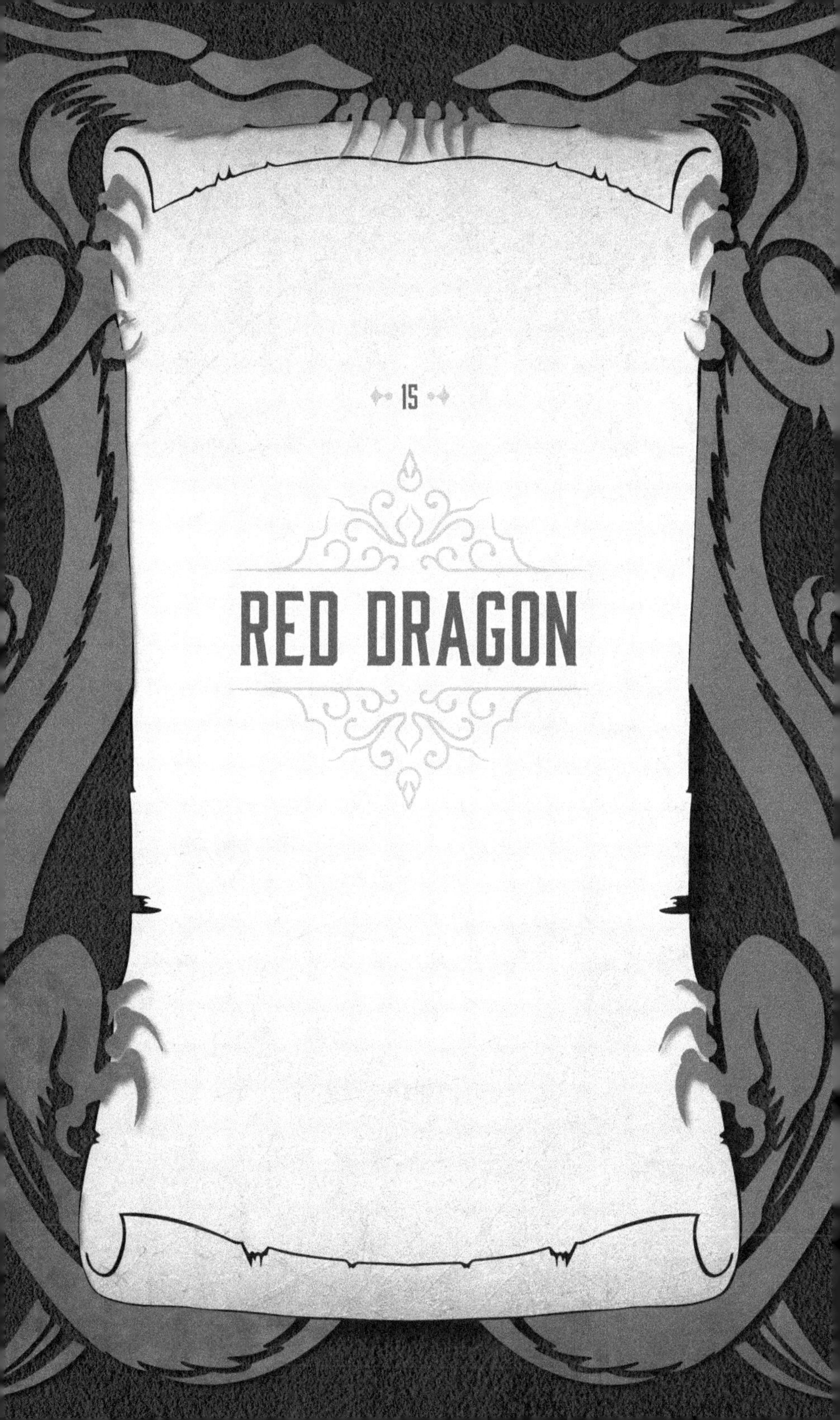

15
RED DRAGON

Within a week, I had keys to the shop in my hand. My head was spinning with the prospect of being in one place in my own shop and building a customer base so that I could apply all the things I had learned on the road. Despite her trying to push me to keep her family in play, I was very clear with the previous owner that I wanted to break all ties with her business and rename the shop. I paid her for the contents and the business, such as it was, and took my legal contract to the landlord and the city offices to change it over. The landlord didn't care; he lived on site and liked to snoop, but all he said was, no drugs. I didn't do drugs so that was easy.

The city applications for business licenses and permits and legal business names were a different story. Germany is a huge wallowing bureaucratic machine and I was sent from one office to another until I had been to all twelve and was back at reception. I was then sent back to the first one. Travelers joked that trees stood up straight when you drove across the border to Germany, because they were so rigid with everything, black and white rules only, no grey areas. Tattooing was apparently a grey area and tattooing had not been registered in Neustadt previously. Not surprisingly, there was no business license or permit to change over either, so I started from the ground up. There was no health department requirement at that time, but I went there anyway and invited them to come by. Later, in the '90s, insurance would be required as the tattoo tidal wave swept the country. The only company that would issue million-dollar indemnities for the landlord was in London, England and their rates were crazy.

The shop was in an old stone building on the main road into Neustadt an der Weinstrasse (there are many Neustadts in Germany, it means new city) from Kaiserslautern where there was an American military base. Rammstein, Landstuhl, Bitburg and Baumholder bases were tucked on this side of the French border a little further out. North was Mannheim, South was Karlsruhe. Neustadt was a smaller town of maybe 50,000 but I really didn't want to be in a city. I've never been a fan of cities, and this was easily accessible from more heavily populated places. There was a large parking lot close to the shop. It had a heavy wooden door with a glass pane in the top half of it, and a bell that tinkled when someone walked in. The two big picture windows on either side of the door were single-pane old lead and rattled as traffic went by. There was an old iron ring hitching post attached to the stone wall by the entrance and I would joke that it was for hitching up client's children. They mostly didn't think it was funny, but it did segway nicely into the conversation that children had no place in tattoo shops. Other than mine, there were no other storefronts for a few hundred yards. It wasn't perfect but it was a start. There was at least a good spot to hang an easily seen sign out front.

The interior consisted of a front room, which was an open space of about 300 square feet and an entryway stepping down into a smaller back room where there was a sink. The short hallway leading out the back door had a small bathroom on one side and a storage space on the other, with a small work shelf that would be perfect for making needles. There was more than enough room for one person to work comfortably with space for a waiting area. The back area was great for drawing and painting and sterilizing. In the front, I split a third off to one side of the main door with a pony wall so that I could work, keep an eye on the customers and answer questions at the same time. Anything left unattended long enough could be stolen because tattoo-related gear was so hard to get. Portfolios, or even just a couple of photos, were high on the list for thieves who could claim them to be their own work. This included flash books and, obviously, the machines and anything easily accessible in the work area. I installed a wall of blued sheet copper halfway down the pony wall to give the workstation some privacy and had a yin-yang design cut into it at eye level so I could see who was coming in the door. My equipment was in a shelving unit with doors, the color bottles and needles and tubes laid out in it. Everything was easily accessed from a seated position. I had inherited a barber chair for the clients from the previous owner. Directed lighting was installed in my area and above the counter where the flash books sat on the wall facing the door. A couch with a table and some magazines for people to look at while they waited. My portfolio sat next to me on the pony wall. It was a fully functional one-person setup and I would always be able to find the scissors! I had made mental notes on the layouts of shops where I had worked and they generally had this system of a customer space well separated from the tattoo artists, so no one could meander among the work areas. It made it seem more special for the client to come back into the space where magic was made and meant I could interact with lookers and potential tattoo buyers while working, without wondering what was going on behind me. I even put bar mirrors in the corners.

Friends had helped me set all this up. Everyone wanted to see the ideas I had brought in from my travels overseas. It was a far cry from my old small van with its battery system and field 'clave. The new electric autoclave and stencil machines gleamed in their corners, and the little American power pack sat proudly on my station next to the shop phone and stack of business cards. I had scraped together some flash books from copies I had made on the road, or that friends had given to me. People had given me paintings and even some dragon statues for the shop.

I decided to name it Red Dragon Tattoo after the tattoo on my upper right arm, the color red symbolizing vitality and energy. Clients and friends would soon start bringing me dragons from all over the world. I was very excited to hear the machines buzzing in my new shop, and I can't really describe the emotion I had having finally gotten this far in the trade that had seemed so unreachable just a few years before. My helpers and I plastered the town with flyers, gave business cards to people in bars and set a grand opening day. It was a great success and when everybody had gone home, I sat in my little shop and got ready for Show Time!

Business was good pretty much from the first day. Tramp-stamps, tribal bands, barbed wire armbands, tiny roses for the ladies. People were intrigued. News spread like wildfire that you could get a professional tattoo from a woman who had traveled the world and worked alongside the tattoo artists from the magazines. To me, it had all been a path of self-directed apprenticeship and learning, but I quickly understood that was a strong selling point. I took out an ad in the Yellow Pages next to Peter's Tattoo Studio, Mannheim and sent a business card to *Easyriders Tattoo* and *International Tattoo* magazines for their advertising section. I cut photos of different tattoos to fit into the two red dragons that framed the top two-thirds of the card as a way to showcase my work, different styles of tattoo for each edition. Photos of tattoos were taken on film of course, and I waited excitedly for the rolls to be developed and see if any of the pictures had turned out without glare or not fuzzy. Good ones went in the portfolio. Over-lit tattoos, glare and bad definition were considered by other artists to be hiding mistakes and were frowned upon, plus they just didn't look good. I was always terrible at taking good shots, so half the film roll would be wasted. While I was going through the photos, I sent some to the German shop owners who were planning tattoo conventions this year to be considered for a booth. I was hopeful that I could start on the convention scene on my own merit, not by luck and circumstance…though that would be okay too!

The Dortmund show's organizers got back to me with acceptance for their next international event. I sent them a check for my booth rental and started to airbrush a display banner for my booth on a 4' by 8' canvas.

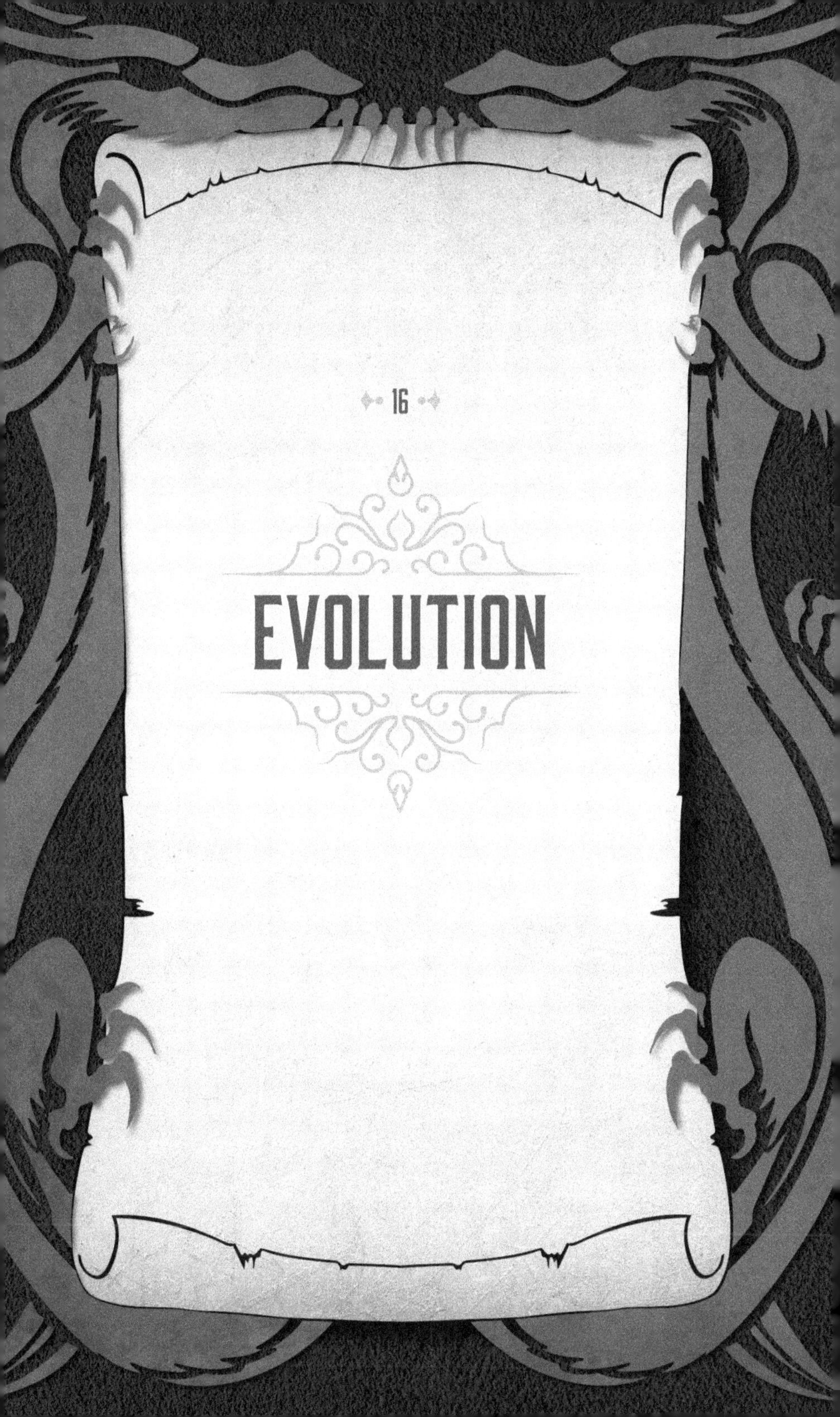
16

EVOLUTION

The very first tattoo convention was in Houston, Texas in 1976 and, as Lyle Tuttle, the legendary Mr Tattoo, was quoted as saying, they changed tattooing forever. Tattoo culture to that point, had mostly been the domain of bikers or was done in prisons and it was definitely not well viewed by the public. These gatherings of like-minded people spawned an exchange of ideas that would travel around the world. As time went by, this counterculture would eventually be embraced by the mainstream, especially as the art form advanced well beyond the very basic designs tailored to sailors, military and bikers. Tattoo enthusiasts and collectors came together to show their colorful skin and there was a wide range from older career-oriented people to punk rockers, skin heads and, of course, bikers. I had a policy that everybody is welcome; just leave your attitude at the door. Sometimes there would be someone's granny being tattooed in the workspace next to me while I tattooed someone that they would have crossed the street to avoid in the real world. These two would laugh and chat and interact; everyone was the same when they were getting a tattoo. It was a beautiful thing.

Case in point, an old man came into my shop one day wearing a tweed suit, and I thought maybe I had blocked his parking space or something. He asked if we could talk in private. Weird but OK. He proceeded to undress completely and show me a complete bodysuit of tattoos, done in the '40s and '50s that he would like to have refreshed. Never judge a book by it's cover! Herr Umhauer. He never gave me his first name. In a different lifetime, he had been an engineer employed by the Nazi war machine. He didn't talk about it. We worked on his bodysuit for years.

It was commonplace to stop people who had good tattoo work on the street or in the store and chat about it and ask who did their work. Tattoos opened conversation without a social barrier. As tattoo artists during that time, we pushed for better standards and good customer service. It made the whole trade look better. The days of 'pick something off the wall, sit down, shut the fuck up and pay me' were becoming a distant memory in most of the shops of the '90s.

The networking potential of the conventions was huge, both as an artist and as a collector. It was something of a challenge to balance functionality of a working tattoo booth and the advertising side of things. If you were traveling far from the shop, it was important not to forget anything, although if equipment failed, you could usually borrow from someone to get you through the weekend or buy from a supplier. This didn't apply to business cards, banners, design books, shop t-shirts and portfolios of course. Setting up your booth well was an opportunity to showcase your art and skill, and your shop. You would be surrounded by other people all doing the same thing, so presentation counted for a lot. The first day of the show, we had a few hours to set up before the public was allowed in, and it was important to not be late. Lines formed outside and as soon as the doors opened, there was no more time to fiddle with the booth set up, unless you wanted to look unprofessional or struggle through the milling crowd with your boxes. Rolling toolboxes were not standard equipment for tattoo artists, so you had to devise a system to carry all your supplies and then set them up on the worktable without it looking like a messy pile of cardboard boxes. You could get creative with boxes hidden under bright cloth, Tupperware for the sterile tools, and anything that really didn't need to be in the way went under the table. You had to have a light, the convention lighting was always dismal, high up on the ceiling and completely useless for working under. Some people built traveling boxes and painted them in wild colors, the front opening out to reveal drawers filled with all the things you needed, even built-in power packs. I was never that slick, but I had a metal toolbox and later a small rolling station that can carry everything, be locked and double as a work surface. Nothing of value could be left overnight, it would be stolen, especially if you left the show floor early. Everyone carried their machines in small gun or camera cases, they went with you everywhere.

The big hand-painted shop banner went on the back wall and design books, portfolio and cards on the front table. The booth layout has not changed over the years, the big names and international artists get the front spaces right inside the main door as they provide a large draw for the show and need to be easy to find. The rest of us fill the rows side by side in between. If you're lucky, you get a cushy corner or end cap. The worst place to be is next to the loudspeakers wherever they are, or by the stage where the public crowd in to watch the competitions and the entertainment, blocking access to the front of your space. Random beer cups left half full sitting on your precious design books, ready to be spilled, or half eaten food left like an afterthought. It's always a good idea to have at least one helper to keep an eye on things while you work. I'm a firm believer from my traveling years that anything not nailed down or supervised will be gone. It's hard to shake!

1995, the third year for Dortmund, and tattoo artists came from all over the world to this one. Tony Bennett was selling supplies and working with Chris Cougar and Ron Ackers, both longtime English tattooers. We talked about joining forces for future events, and we did. They would come to my shop, and we would go all over Germany together for the rest of the decade. They liked having a German translator and someone who could navigate all the nasty food. Plus, we had a lot of laughs, piss-taking as only the English can. I was sitting next to Ron in Berlin when the girl he was tattooing passed out and slid with a thud to the concrete floor. Not missing a beat, he leaned down over her and continued tattooing. I stopped him and picked her up and dusted her off. We didn't let him forget it. I added a small fan to the necessary for shows list. The number of bodies made it incredibly hot and sticky in those places.

Among the better known European artists at the time were

Tin-Tin, Mick from Zurich, Luke Atkinson and Bernie Luther, (whose freehand technique of drawing a red pen base line and then refining it with a blue pen before tattooing the design, I totally stole and still use now, even thought the trust in the freehand process has long since been annihilated by TV shows.)

Fiona Long, an English woman with a shock of blond hair, was fresh back from the States with awards from the Mad Hatter's Tea Party, a show in Maine. In 1988, she had been able to use an English government program called Employment Training to learn how to tattoo. In 1995, she opened her own shop, Feline Tattoo in Sheffield. She would go on to be a darling of the European conventions and win many more awards for her bright, clean and artistic tattooing. An up-and-coming German tattoo artist, Sabine Gaffron, would also rapidly become a star. A mostly self-taught Berliner who had started tattooing in 1990, she had been inspired by meeting Bernie Luther on the Berlin squat scene. She picked up scraps of information from unhelpful male tattooers in shops. Her first big break onto the convention scene at the 1992 Berlin show led to her own tattoo shop, opened in 1995, and much recognition on the international circuit. These women were hugely inspiring to me, although we never really got a chance to know each other. We were all insanely busy on the showroom floor and off doing different things in the evening. Everyone broke down their spaces and left on Sunday; we all vanished until next time.

Other female artists were beginning to show up on the scene; Genziana from Italy, Teresa Gordon from England, Heidi Hay from Sweden and Jacqueline Spoerle from Switzerland, whose tribal style tattoos were super crisp and clean and black. It was good to see so many women artists coming up, but we were still way in the minority, and you'd still hear onlookers making comments about how they'd never get tattooed by a woman. That would begin to change as more of us won awards and were featured in magazines. The TV reporters who filmed around the show spotlighted women artists, because we were a big curiosity in this male dominated profession, as did the local newspaper reports. In 1995, a Swiss newspaper wrote an article about me entitled "In a Man's Profession". We obviously weren't there yet.

Paul Booth's black-and-grey demon style was a hit in Europe, and I bought his flash for my shop. Henning Jorgensen from Denmark, Hanky Panky from Amsterdam, Marco Leoni from Italy, Darren Stares from England, Mike Davis from San Francisco, my old friend Crazy Ace and many others were tattooing at Dortmund's international convention in 1995; they would all become a staple at the European conventions. Meanwhile tattooers came together from all over the world and talked about our main obsession, tattooing, and all the new equipment we were using and whose colors might be better, trade secrets that are now a thing of the past among recognized professionals. I translated between French and German and English and Spanish, sometimes all four languages at once, depending on the company. At the end of these sessions, my head would feel like a washing machine of words, but I enjoyed being able to make the bridge for everybody. After the show was over for the day, everybody partied like rockstars, and we all had fun. The staff of the 4-star hotels we stayed in were a bit worried when all the tattooed people first checked in, but after a weekend of high bar tabs and good tips, they came to appreciate our visits. Sunday was usually a bad day to have the first appointment as a client at a show!

The German public ate it all up. They started cutting holes in their clothing to show off their art pieces and getting crazy piercings and bigger tattoos that they happily displayed in contests, which were a daily event. Some artists brought their own clients to enter the competitions, mostly for Best of Day or Best of Show, which had to be a piece done on site. They would work on these all weekend. The daily categories ranged from small to large in all the styles. There was also a category for best tattooed female as women began to get much bigger tattoos. They were judged by whichever tattoo artist was not looking too busy or sometimes by celebrities like the Swiss artist H.R.Giger, famous for his work on the film, *Alien.* Giger art pieces were a popular tattoo design in Germany. He autographed one that I had done with gold pen on the client's skin, and later I would go and visit his work studio in Heidelberg and get to know his 'shadow painter.' Giger was a very eccentric man.

It wasn't easy to win at the big international shows, and there was always a lot of grumbling about favoritism especially when the hot chick in a bikini won a category with a tiny tattoo, and an even tinier bikini. Awards looked good on the wall of the shop though. They came in various styles, everything from large trophies to carved plaques and everybody pushed the envelope a little harder to bring one home. Sometimes customers would win awards for your work at shows you didn't attend and bring them to the shop. Eventually I insisted that they keep them, they had, after all, sat through the tattoo and paid for it. I do wish I had kept my only Best of Show plaque I won in Vancouver, Canada, though. It was carved into a thick glass standing piece and beautiful. Organizers would eventually make awards for both collector and artist, which I personally think is more fair.

There was never a shortage of clients at the shows, no need to book anybody because last year's customers would be back for more. Of course, the big names were booked but that just meant more work for the rest of us. It felt like potential clients would never stop coming. People started to collect artists' signatures on the convention posters. Local rock bands, mostly awful, played loudly throughout the weekend. The buzz of tattoo machines filled the venue. People drank the place dry. It was a lot like Carnival. 'Curiosities' like the Leopard Man on display in a cage, leopard print tattooed all over his body, 97 % coverage, they said; his teeth were filed to points. The rest of the time, his name was Tom. He lived alone on a small island in Scotland. The Enigma from the States, better known as Puzzle Man to the uninitiated, showed up from time to time, blue puzzle pieces all over his body and implanted coral growing as horns from his forehead. Isobel Varley from England, who was very heavily tattooed, liked to proudly display a bright red devil head decorating her vagina; she had been a bored housewife in a different life. Rocky from Hamburg with his tall mohawk and heavily tattooed and pierced face wowed the crowd.

The attending public started to look wilder and as the popularity of piercings grew, so did their presence. Men with split penises, held together by multiple small ball-closure rings; metal balls implanted in the testicles dragging them down to the knees; nipple piercings hanging to the waist with the weight of the jewelry; huge, stretched ears; split tongues; metal implants under the skin. All the curious underworld of the Dutch and Belgian sex clubs. The British company Wildcat, known for their extreme piercing and large jewelry selection sold out quickly at every show, you couldn't buy their products anywhere else. Tattooers didn't have much respect for piercing, it was so non-permanent compared to what we did, and the piercers were strangely arrogant considering they just poked holes in people. But we couldn't ignore the rise in its popularity or the bondage-gear-wearing or naked, heavily pierced and branded freaks that began to wander through the showroom floor. New magazines appeared in France and Italy and Germany. Newspapers, radio and TV wanted interviews. The explosion in popularity of tattooing in Europe was a huge colorful freight train and it was a wild ride for those of us who were on it.

It was great publicity for the shop, business boomed, and I began to attend more conventions in cities all over Europe, Madrid, Barcelona, Vienna, Amsterdam, Berlin, Stuttgart, Munich, Brussels, Geneva, Zurich, Bologna, Lausanne, Hamburg, Bordeaux, Dunstable, London. The travel became a blur. There was never time to be a tourist. Arrive, work, leave. I was working at at least two conventions a month. I would later meet and befriend the American tattooer Bert Rodriguez, who had apprenticed to Davy Jones in Oakland in the early '60s and, as was mentioned about him in a roast, if there was a show going on that would have him, he would tattoo there. I knew the feeling. Sometimes the situations were curious, like a Hamburg show which was held in a hall with balconies surrounding the stage and a main floor where most of the artists were set up. I left on the second day because of the dry ice pumping off the stage and into my balcony booth. I couldn't see and they refused to turn it off. The smaller local shows were not always well advertised. The motorcycle rallies would sometimes abruptly come to an end because a large biker club would arrive and start fighting with the members of another club. Police would come and shut the event down. But none were ever as uneventful as that Copenhagen show in 1994.

One of the best conventions I remember attending was Munich in 1995, hosted by Tattoo Sohne. It was in an old ballroom in the center of Munich, there was an upstairs gallery and a main floor. The lighting was amazing, and the space itself was architecturally grand. Sohne threw a welcoming dinner for all the artists on the first night at a traditional Bavarian Inn next door to the show. He said that without us, there was no show, and he was the only organizer I had personally met to acknowledge that in such a giving way and I think a lot of people would agree with me.

Mao, the Spanish tattooer who had so impressed me in Cádiz, had been the godfather of tattooing in his country making many international friends and connections and hosting two great shows in Spain in the cities of Madrid and Barcelona, to which he brought Polynesian hand tappers Purotu, Chime and Roonui who had between them revived Marquesan and Tahitian tatau tradition. Tribal style tattooing now began to take off all over Europe. Traditional tribal artists from Borneo, Samoa and Polynesia began displaying their craft at most conventions. I'm not sure who was more culture shocked, them or us. It must have been a lot for them to come to Europe, and especially to the States from their small island communities. Other than the language barrier, they seemed to be having a damn good time.

As the years passed, and the money flowed, big conventions would begin to appear, promoted by non-tattoo artists and the quality standards were dropped so that over a hundred booths could be crammed in, whereas before there may have only been 50. They charged accordingly. The trade was becoming an industry.

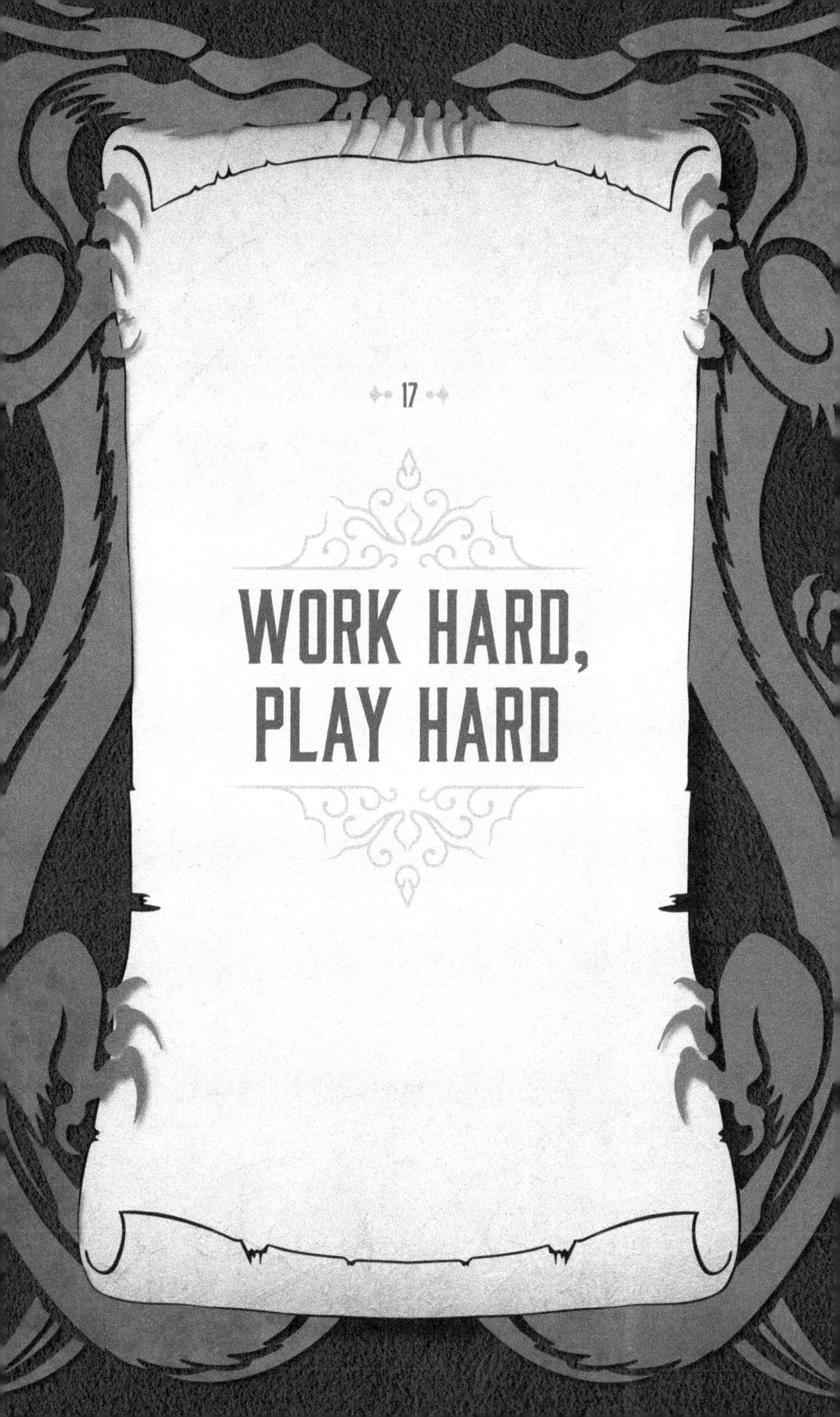

17
WORK HARD,
PLAY HARD

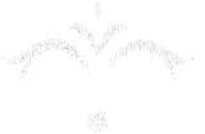

y little shop was beginning to fill up with everything from wooden carved dragon statues and competition awards to commercially available flash design sets that I had bought at the conventions or copied from other tattooers' collections. Much to the dissatisfaction of the artist who sold them (I was one of them), we would each buy a different set, then go to the copy shop, print them off and trade. They were expensive to purchase but in reality, you could make the investment back doing a few designs from a good set. Different styles flowed from the pages. All styles tattooing was my preferred choice, feeling that specializing narrowed things down too much, and eventually you might be tired of doing the same thing every day. I've always loved the variety in a day that might go from a tribal piece to a small cherry to a big Japanese flower. Having art drawn up by different people meant that the treatment of the piece was not the same as I would have done it myself, more challenging to my skill as an artist. I also began to buy reference books on everything from castles to flowers, whatever was available, even just glossy photo collections. Fantasy art by illustrators like Boris Vallejo and the legendary Frank Frazetta was extremely popular. There still were not many books available directly related to tattooing, but I had as many of those as I could find including Ed Hardy's *Dragon Tattoo Design* book. I did a lot of dragons.

I drew custom designs for my clients, spending hours to get the right fit. Very often, I would then freehand the design from my reference to give it a better flow on the body. The pieces grew in size and degree of difficulty and increased the number of sessions needed, but this was welcome because I could scrutinize what was already healed when I did the next session. This was the only way to see how bright the colors were or how well the machines were pushing the ink. The strength of the black was also important. I would pour the Pelikan ink into a dedicated coffee pot and let it sit overnight on warm to evaporate the water. It worked well. Pelikan would eventually stop selling to the tattoo market when they found out that we were using it in the skin. Allergic reactions could mean lawsuits for the manufacturer. Permapro from the States was the best color formula we had ever seen.

I stuck mostly to the same needle groupings of three for a basic line, five or seven round for a sculpted line where needed, and a seven magnum for the shade and color. Each needle grouping had a machine tuned just for that particular grouping. I changed machines as I progressed through the piece, lines to shading to color. I bought new machines at the conventions but was always loyal to my Mickey Sharpz for the most part. They were the lightest to my hand and functioned well as workhorses;

a long time between replacing springs and having to tune them up again was a good thing with a heavy workload. I always had a back-up machine standing by in case one of the three should have a problem that I couldn't troubleshoot quickly, such as a broken coil wire or a blown capacitor. Machine won't work, try another one. If that works, it's the machine not the power pack or the clip cord/foot-switch assembly. Is the needle bar cinched down too tight with the elastic band? Is the needle bent too far down on the bar? Is there something between the spring and the contact screw? Did the contact screw come loose? All these were easy fixes, everything else would have to wait til later. I had 20 machines in my drawer. Every time I looked at them, I thought about how hard it had been to get the first one!

I set up appointments for the majority of my work, not seeing any other way to regulate the flow of traffic. If I had time for a walk-in, I would do it, but for the most part, I couldn't have people walking in for the size and complexity of tattoos that I was doing. This also meant that I could be away working at a show and not worry about lost business. People would wait, as long as they had an appointment set up. There was no emphasis on needing a deep meaning for your chosen tattoo, although there was the occasional request for hidden initials in tribal or other designs or just way too much content in a tiny tattoo. If it's important enough for you to put a name on your body, make sure it's legible, I would say. Spelling was always problematic even for names that should have been a no-brainer, a bit like anniversary dates and birthdays. I always had the customer write it down exactly as they wanted it. Once, a man who wanted his wife's name, Marion in a banner and was very happy with his tattoo, came back quickly to tell me that he had spelt it wrong and that her name was spelt M-A-R-I-A-N-N-E. I asked how long he had been married? Twelve years. I'm guessing he slept on the couch for a while. Sometimes, I would strategically place the name somewhere easy to cover, especially if I knew any of the back story. When I was covering up names, I would ask the reason that they had been applied in the first place; often it was to try and patch up a failing relationship, a proof of true love. One woman had her abusive husband's name covered and reapplied so many times that I refused to do it anymore. He came by and yelled at me, calling me a stupid bitch and saying I had no right to tell her no. I kicked him out. I always reserved the right to refuse service.

I began to work a lot with cover-up requests. Germany was, at the time, a place where people who had bad tattoos wanted them covered with something not much bigger than the existing work. My process used the art style *'trompe l'oeuil'* to hide the old design and use the existing lines as much as possible in the new piece, distracting the eye with use of open space and bright color. That way the cover-ups weren't huge and ridiculously black. A man came to me one day with a tattoo that was supposed to be a Viking head. It was only the outline, but it was a disaster. The story was that he had gone into a shop in Hamburg that was very clean and shiny (because it was brand new) and the tattoo applicator had fallen hard on his slippery tile floor after spilling the rinse water and broken his arm and been hauled off in an ambulance. When the customer washed the big black smudge off his arm at his hotel room, he was hor-rified. He needed it fixed before his wife came home from a trip. I told him to look on the bright side, if it had been finished, it would have really been hard to cover up.

There's an American Old School saying that we use for extremely busy, hyper-detailed tattoo requests; 'ten pounds of shit in a five-pound bag'. It doesn't make for a legible tattoo that will hold well over time. The test of a really good tattoo design is if it can be easily recognized if you hold the design up five feet away. Anything else will blur quickly. Look at a tiny fairy design after six months and the face will be a smudge. The skin medium is not the same as paper or canvas. The devil isn't in the details at that point; the devil IS the details. Japanese, tribal and traditional American styles all age well and at the time, we were trying to apply parts of their technical process to everything. You could put detail into a strong clean design as long as that wasn't what held it all together. Solid black out-lines were a must. Blood outline or color lines were not going to hold the tattoo for long.

I didn't do a huge amount of flash tattoos, but they were a good way to get the customer's thought process for their idea stimulated. Later there would be very popular design sets from Cherry Creek that the public loved and couldn't be talked out of. You had to be a good artist to navigate them and redraw all those eagles that looked like they had just flown into a brick wall. The Brazilian artist Mauricio also produced a lot of flash, which was very popular, and his art was strong, his fantasy designs bold and solid. Tribal and Celtic design sets came out from Eus in

Holland and Leo Zulueta. And there was J.D.Crowe's Official Tattoo Brand as a long-time staple for every design you could imagine. I bought it all.

My hundred tubes came in very handy as the ultrasonic cleaner would fill quickly to overflowing. I put the used needles and tubes into it after each tattoo and it buzzed all day. Every day began with scrubbing and cleaning these tubes with a bottle brush to get all the ink residue out from the inside of them. I would sterilize the used needles and break them off into a Sharps Container. The bars were then sterile for reloading and the needles were sterile in case anyone got stuck with them, because we threw the containers into the regular waste bins. The tubes were put in sterilizer bags. These bags had to be cut to size from a roll and sealed into pouches with a little heat machine that would burn your hands and leave holes in the pouches if you weren't fast enough. The arrival of self-seal pouches was very welcome. The autoclave ran while the floor got mopped, the toilet was cleaned and the rubbish was taken out, then to the job of making needles for the day, listening to the voice messages, calling people back, ordering supplies. If you weren't at least an hour early to the shop for all this, you were late. I suspect that's why a lot of shops began to take apprentices. I toyed with that idea but came home from a convention to find that an apprentice hopeful had tried to start a back piece while I was gone. That was the end of that. Doing all the grunt work was just part of the job, but then came a ten- or twelve-hour workday.

Tattooing may appear to the inexperienced eye as easy, just drawing pictures all day long, but when you do it intensively, it becomes mentally draining. The changing faces and mentalities of the clients are a lot to manage too. It's hard to go from talking to an old lady, say, to an energetic young mechanic, both of whom want to talk about their interests and you have to converse with them throughout. A lot of people treated their sessions as if they were at the hairdresser and downloaded all kinds of stories and different complaints. The '90s were before the days of every tattoo requiring a deep and meaningful tale behind it; people just wanted a tattoo. They talked a lot about themselves. It reminded me of the things that barkeeps hear, just more personal. One example, during the application of a small rose tattoo, a woman told me all about how she had killed her husband. He had been abusive throughout their marriage, she said, and when he became so ill that he couldn't move, she had overmedicated him to death. It seemed valid. I never saw her again.

It was a lot to absorb and hard to tune out. Add to that the intense concentration on work and at the end of the day, I sometimes couldn't remember where I had parked my bike that morning. I finally decided that I was going to need to find some counter help or another artist or both. The problem with a growing small business is that it's like a small child that needs a lot of nurturing and then can quickly grow to become a monster you can't control. When you should be celebrating your success, you are worried about how to manage it. At that point, you look to expansion and that is a whole other level of difficult to manage.

I had been reading Richard Bach's book *Illusions: The Adventures of a Reluctant Messiah* about flying barnstormer planes and thought that skill might come in handy during an apocalypse. I decided to take flying lessons and think about what to do next with the shop from several thousand feet.

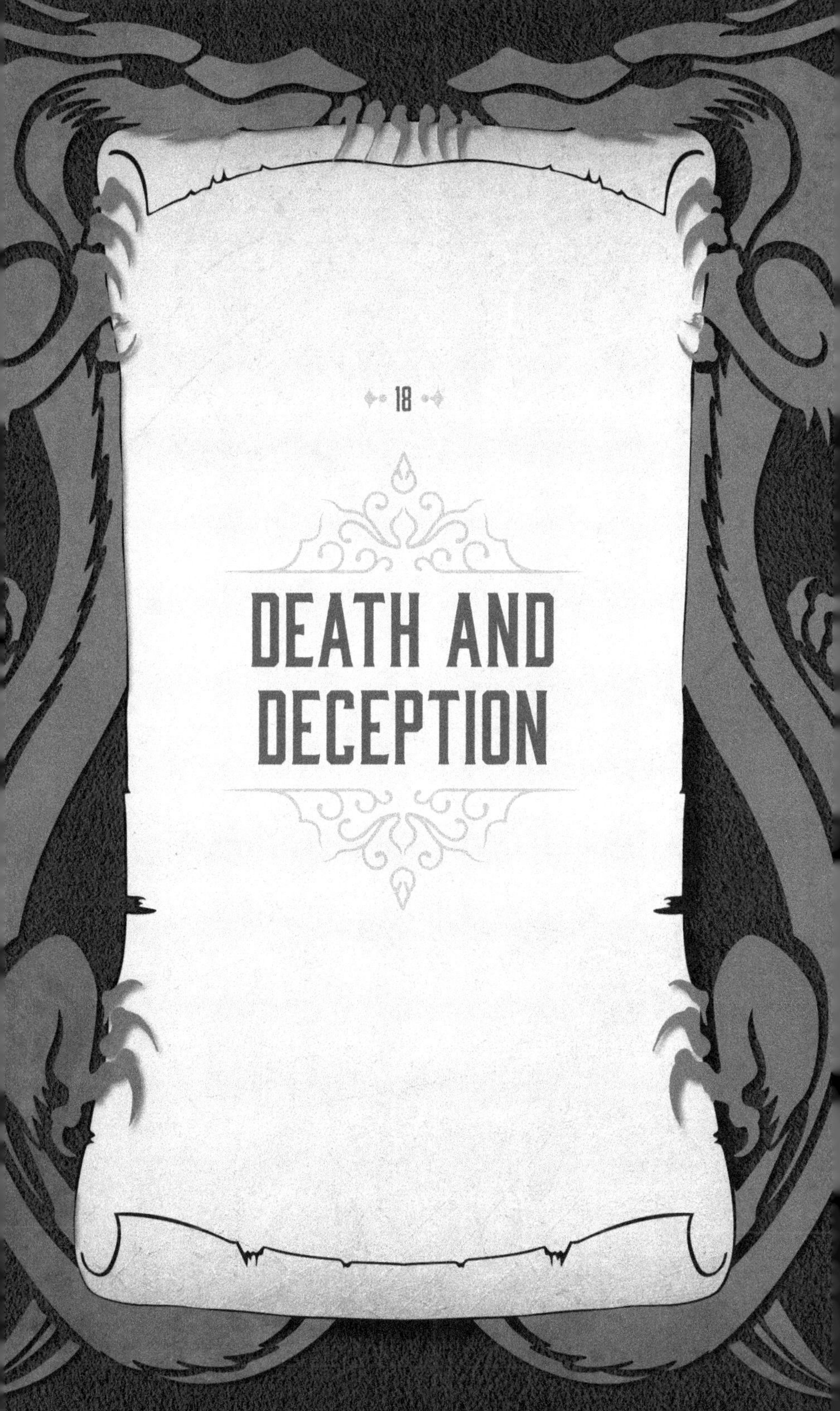

18

DEATH AND
DECEPTION

The shop doorbell jingled one day and in walked a scruffy hippy type who was covered in black dotwork tattoos. He was English and his name was Xed LeHead. He was looking for some work if he could have a few days sitting in. He said he didn't really know how to use machines, but he'd give it a go. He had been tattooing by hand for a while and was pretty good at it. He would solder and tie needles to a chopstick and hand poke intricate dot work designs for hours on end. I wasn't really sure if this would ever be a good sell, time would prove me very wrong. I let him use some set-up professional machines and try out for a couple of weeks. He showed me how to hand poke in exchange. Tribal style was very up and coming in Germany in 1998 and the shop clients loved Xed's designs and eccentricities and even the dotwork. Apparently, my new artist had arrived. The shop was quickly becoming too small for us both and so I began to look for a bigger location.

Soon, I had found a new space to rent, and the shop was being put together; a metal dragon burst from the corner above my new station, its wingtips gave the appearance of breaking through the walls either side of the corner. Copper sheet walls heated to create multiple color effects framed off the area where the flash books would be set out on display. It was impressive to look at. The space was well-lit and had enough room for four tattoo stations. Laminate countertop ran the length of the back wall. Only two stations were stocked for now, immediately in view of the entry door which led into a courtyard with a seating area, each decorated with paintings by the respective artists and whatever display they wanted. I bought an electric dentist's chair that raised up and down and laid flat. This was high tech. Big full-length mirrors hung where the clients could access them easily. The waiting area was just inside the entryway faced by a desk for the main counter with its appointment books and phone. Another metal wall made an L with this desk and created the drawing area with its own window. The floor was light tile and there were two sinks, one by the tattoo stations and one in the corner for the cleaning and sterilizing space. We even had a small kitchen. The courtyard led out to the street under the old building which had an apartment above the walkway. It was close in location to the other shop. Definitely a bright, clean and shiny upgrade, I missed the vibe of the smaller space which had been my own for the last three years, but growth seemed to be important in these days of booming business. The new shop remodel hadn't been cheap, but it looked very modern and fresh.

I did have a dilemma with the old shop though; if I let it go, it could easily be taken over by another tattoo business and leech from my hard work building a customer base. I was so far the only game in town, but more and more people were fascinated with the idea of being tattoo artists. Non-tattooers were opening shops and hiring artists as an investment. Money attracts like nothing else, but I don't believe that anyone who is not a tattoo artist should be involved in the running of a tattoo shop and all it's eccentricities. If you don't belong, don't be long!

The Indian Spirit leather and jewelry sales had started to wane on the convention circuit and the family I had bought the shop from were lurking on the fringes, visiting regularly, getting tattooed. I had constantly been warned about their shiesty ways by locals and people who knew their shenanigans well. They were known to be like tinkers, take here and there, give nothing back, move on to the next mark. These were exactly the kind of people who would go behind my back and take over the old studio. I decided to contain the threat and include them in the new business. Ludwigstrasse, the first location would become a piercing studio, the piercing business was very hot now. I sent the mother to Frankfurt to be trained by a professional and stocked the shop with supplies from Wildcat in England. It made a perfect piercing studio. The daughter would be my counter help and personal assistant at the new location.

And so Red Dragon Tattoo grew. I hosted a small local show with Xed and Arno, Dirk from Schwäbisch Hall and my British friends (Chris and Tony from the convention circuit) in coordination with the grand opening. We continued to attend the conventions and I worked local motorcycle rallies, the only place where I would still hear comments like "I would never get tattooed by a bitch." New tattoo magazines had started to publish monthly editions in Germany, France and Italy, their articles on mostly European artists, and the tribal artists from overseas who were ever more popular at the shows. Northern Europe started to lean heavily towards tribal tattoo art and Xed was right there, ready to shine. He would eventually become known as the godfather of dotwork tattooing, his unique geometric style influencing the entire global tattoo community.

Guest artists came on a regular basis; Claudio Benvenuti from Bologna, Italy, Chris Cougar from England and many more. There was plenty of work for everybody, the piercing studio was also very successful. I was published in the French *Tatouage* Magazine under the heading," Mother Never Knew" because my mother had never seen my tattoo collection, which was by now extensive. I was driving regularly to Paris to have my back piece inked by Tin-Tin; a freehand Celtic warrioress which earned multiple best back piece awards at the shows. The German *Taetowiermagazin* published an article on my cover- up work. *Tattoo Life* came to the shop and interviewed Xed and me for a six-page spread; the article made it seem like we were partners, which we were not. I was thrilled to be published but a little miffed that my status as shop owner was not mentioned. That may seem petty, but I can't even begin to describe the amount of work that I had done to create and operate this business and I felt that a little recognition was due. Most of the women on the European circuit had opened their own shops by this point because it was easier than working for men, who tended to take credit for everything and were mostly dismissive of our efforts. I had several men who worked for me over the years insist that without them, I would not have a success-ful business. Xed was actually the first to say this, but only later in our story, when everyone was overwhelmed and running towards burnout due to our massive workload. Success has its own price. Everywhere I went some stranger knew me, even once in Madrid airport. I didn't care for it. I have never been a people person. I'm good at putting a mask on and being in the moment for Show Time, as I call going to work, but I'd much rather be somewhere quiet on my boat.

I was definitely getting burned out due to overwork. I still flew small planes and was having a big flirtation with American cars, which was quite frustrating due to lack of available parts and often the orders that arrived from the States by mail after six weeks were not the right ones. We could buy cars from American servicemen who were going home but had no direct access to spares other than a catalog and a phone number. I was driving a '79 Camaro and amused myself roaring through the narrow streets of old cities like Paris, the engine rumble setting off car alarms right, left and center. I had a sticker across the back window with the shop name on it and was having a hotrod built from a 1948 Chevrolet, installing a 392 HEMI engine for street-racing competition. I went to Hockenheim racetrack with the car builders running a 1957 Thunderbird as a Super Competition dragster; you can't have more fun in 8.7 seconds, I promise! It was a lot of fun and a good distraction from work despite being outrageously expensive. German Autobahns famously didn't have a speed limit outside of the cities, and I would ride my Suzuki GSX1100 like a bat out of hell until the day some arsehole in a Porsche tried to force me into the outside shoulder at 120 mph. I didn't crash the bike, although I was a bit rattled. But none of this silliness was enough to settle my mind, and I wasn't interested in finding a boyfriend, despite numerous applications for the job. Life on my own was good. Travel was on my mind again. The shop had a good crew and could take care of itself for a few weeks, I wanted to go somewhere I had never been before and have a vacation.

I decided to go to the local bookstore and check out the travel section, and there, I found a book with a stone temple on the front cover and pictures of carvings on stelae in an art form I didn't recognize. The world of the ancient Maya in the jungles of southern Mexico looked like a very curious place, and that's where I wanted to go. The travel agent was less than enthusiastic; she insisted that it might be dangerous for a single female to be that far out in the middle of nowhere in a foreign country, but I told her to book me anyway. The journey would take days, flying via Dallas, Texas and Mexico City to a town called Villahermosa in the Yucatán where I would have to take a taxi to Palenque, Chiapas and my hotel. Thirty-six hours of just flying. As it turned out, the airline forgot my luggage in Dallas, and I had to stay overnight in Mexico City waiting for it. The flight to Villahermosa was redirected to Tuxtla Gutiérrez due to the forest fires around Palenque, and the only way from there was in a bush plane with cracked windows and wings held together by duct tape; a local pilot hired by some businessmen in a hurry. I was glad I could speak Spanish and snuck on with them. Four days after leaving Germany, I arrived in the smoke-filled village of Palenque and stayed for a month. I toured the temples in their various sites, fascinated by Mayan art, and sat on top of one tattooing myself by hand, far from the bustle of the shop and the demands of customers.

Back in Germany, the buzz on the street worried about the upcoming millennium because when the numbers rolled to '00, the world might end. I paid the pile of bills and got back into the daily grind. The mice hadn't been playing too much while the cat was away, but I did have a new guest artist, Mark B from England who was a friend of Xed. He was a solid tattooer, he could stay. Not long after that, my father called the shop and asked me to come to Northern England and visit; Mother had cancer. I hadn't had much contact with my parents who disapproved of my traveling adventures and my tattoo career, but as an adopted child, I felt I couldn't refuse to help him as he had once helped me by giving me a home. Plus, my dad was a good human being and I loved him for it. And so began a long drawn out six months of working at my shop during the week and flying to England on the weekends to help my dad learn how to cope with running a household and caring for Mother. I was distracted but the bills were paid, and business continued as usual, Xed and Mark holding down the fort. A friend moved down from northern Germany to help at the front desk and with the daily running of things. I worked as much as possible. One night, my dad called late and told me the hospice nurse had been called and I should come as soon as I could, he was crying. I dropped everything and headed for Northern England. Mother passed away on February 13th, 2000. I was caught up in the paperwork details and consoling my dad, but after the funeral, which was two weeks later, I told him I had to get back to my business. By now, I was getting worried about it despite the daily phone updates. It is a solid fact that employees don't treat a business with the same care as the person who has built it and runs it, and it cannot be left unsupervised for too long. Putting a shop together is easy, keeping it together is the hard part.

The next morning, I walked into the piercing shop to meet the piercer and pick up the money drop. Her husband was there and moved behind me to stand in the back hallway. They were acting very strangely. She then announced in no uncertain terms that seeing as I was apparently not interested in running the businesses properly anymore and never around, she would be taking them over and I would work for her. I was shocked to the point of almost speechless. I said, "Fuck you, I just buried my mother." Her husband moved quickly behind me and said aggressively," You don't talk to my wife that way." I answered, "Get the fuck out of my way" and he grabbed me by the arm and told me I'd do well to listen. I was furious but honestly not surprised. These people were indeed snakes. I tore loose and walked out.

I needed to process what was happening. I am famous for my temper but losing my shit right now didn't seem like it would be the best idea. At the tattoo shop, the daughter was sullen and silent, obviously on board with the family plan. Mark and Xed were working, they didn't appear to know anything. I tried to silence my mind whilst working on my tattoo client for the day, longing for the times when all this had been so much simpler, wondering where it had all gone wrong. I was suddenly overwhelmingly sick of it all. I was damned if I was going to let anybody take what I had built away from me by backing me into a corner.

In the coming days, I played along with the family's plan, saying I would do the paperwork on Monday. I refuse to name these people because naming a person gives them power according to the Native Americans; I will despise them forever. Their son, wearing his brand-new one percent motorcycle club colors hovered at the shop, pretending to be visiting his sister. I refused to be intimidated, and I was too tired to fight. Time was of the essence. That night, I sold the tattoo shop to Mark with official legal papers and a clear understanding of what was going on. I emptied the supplies from the piercing studio into a box and gave the key to the landlord with a check for the inconvenience; he didn't want anything more to do with the family anyway. I backed up to the tattoo shop and loaded my tattoo equipment, my books, my dragon collection and a few mementos, and left the key. The contents of my apartment I walked away from, including the box full of competition awards in a closet.

I left Germany like a thief in the night, I had stolen my freedom back. I wasn't even curious about what happened next, although I would like to have been a bug on the wall the next day. The Red Dragon had flown.

It was time to get back to what I do best, traveling and tattooing.

ABOUT THE AUTHOR

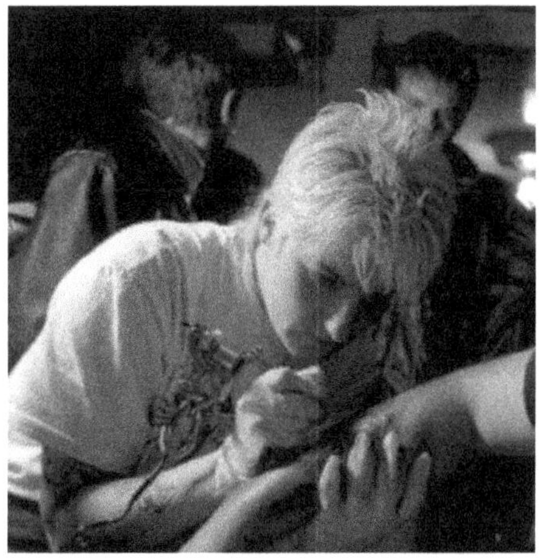

Pym Avery is a professional multi-award-winning tattoo artist. She began to teach herself the trade in 1987 at a time when no one would entertain women as apprentices in this heavily male dominated world. Consequently, she traveled throughout Europe in her van to acquire tattooing experience and enough skill to convince a shop to hire her. Her quest took her into the tattoo convention world of the '90s, the decade when tattooing as an art form exploded into the public consciousness. She opened her first tattoo shop in 1995.

Pym has owned several tattoo studios over the years, but now prefers to work independently at tattoo conventions or as a guest artist by appointment only, allowing more time for commissioned paintings and writing. She travels and works mostly in the United States and resides in Tucson, AZ when not on her sailboat in Mexico.